A CHRISTIAN'S GUIDE TO JUDAISM

Studies in
Judaism and Christianity

Exploration of Issues in the
Contemporary Dialogue Between
Christians and Jews

Editor in Chief for
Stimulus Books
Helga Croner

Editors
Lawrence Boadt, C.S.P.
Helga Croner
Rabbi Leon Klenicki
Kevin A. Lynch, C.S.P.
Dennis McManus
Dr. Ann Riggs
Rabbi Leonard Schoolman

A STIMULUS BOOK

A CHRISTIAN'S GUIDE TO JUDAISM

Michael Lotker

[handwritten signature]
561-842-7542
Sep 2016

A STIMULUS BOOK

PAULIST PRESS ◆ NEW YORK ◆ MAHWAH, N.J.

Cover design by Trudi Gershenov

Book design by Sally A. Szymanski and Theresa M. Sparacio

Glossary pronunciation guide taken from the *JPS Dictionary of Jewish Words* by Joyce Eisenberg and Ellen Scolnic (Jewish Publication Society, 2001) with permission.

Library of Congress Cataloging-in-Publication Data

Lotker, Michael.
    A Christian's guide to Judaism / Michael Lotker.
       p.   cm. — (A Stimulus book)
    Includes bibliographical references and index.
    ISBN 0-8091-4232-5 (alk. paper)
    1. Judaism. 2. Christianity and other religions—Judaism. 3. Judaism—Relations—Christianity. I. Title.

BM562 .L68 2004
296'.02'427—dc22

20030

Published by Paulist Press
997 Macarthur Boulevard
Mahwah, New Jersey 07430

www.paulistpress.com

Printed and bound in the
United States of America

Contents

For George and Grace Lotker, of blessed memory,
who gave me my Judaism,

For Carol, who insisted that I nurture it,

For Howie, Stefanie, and Andrea,
who inspire me to help repair the world,

And for Sonia, who sustained me through the worst
and leads me to the best.

Acknowledgments

Space prevents me from properly thanking all those who helped me on the spiritual journey that led to this book. I am grateful to my rabbis, Alan Greenbaum, Edward Zerin, Larry Kushner, and Mordecai Finley, for their insights and comfort over the years. How many times did they tell me "you should really be a rabbi"? Who knew that they were right!

At the Hebrew Union College–Jewish Institute of Religion (HUC–JIR), my rabbinical school, I was showered with the wisdom of scholars and their texts. I am especially grateful to Rabbi Richard Levy, director of the Los Angeles School of Rabbinical Studies, for his mentorship, his warmth, his encouragement, and his careful and thoughtful review of this manuscript. So many other HUC–JIR teachers and rabbis have left their mark on my soul and thought; David Ellenson (president of the College-Institute), Lewis Barth (dean of the Los Angeles campus), Reuven Firestone (director of the Jerome H. Loucheim School of Judaic Studies and Edgar F. Magnin School of Graduate Studies and my thesis advisor). William Cutter, Rivka Dori, Tamara Cohn Eskenazi, Steven Passamaneck, and Adam Rubin have, in the past five years, challenged and stretched me. Rabbi Michael Goldberg encouraged me to begin this project and, along with Rabbi Michael Klein-Katz, provided insightful comments on early drafts. Of course, any errors in the text are fully mine and not those of the people mentioned above.

It's not so easy to reenter graduate school in your fifties; my days and evenings (and often late nights and weekends) were enriched by my fellow students. Both in Jerusalem and in Los Angeles, Yossi Carron has been unselfish with his love and support. Suzanne Singer provided precious insights to this manuscript and has always been there for me with good advice and a listening ear. They will both make wonderful rabbis.

I am indebted to my publisher, Father Lawrence Boadt, who saw the promise of a book of this kind and who has been more than patient and encouraging during its creation. I have often remarked how wonderful it is to have a priest as publisher; he always forgave me when I was late on my deadlines!

As I mention in the introduction, this book was written during my wife's battle with Huntington's Disease. I would never have had the strength to endure these years without the friendship of Jill and Len Polan, Alan Warshaw, and, my business partner and friend, Bill Rassman. Beyond these closest friends I have been supported and encouraged by scores of friends and colleagues with whom I've studied, prayed, laughed, and cried. Acknowledging each of them would require another book.

Most of all, I want to acknowledge the continuous support and encouragement of my brothers and their wonderful wives, Jack and Charlotte Lotker and David and Eleanor Lotker, my brother- and sister-in-law Robin and Ed Roffman, and my mother-in-law who is also my stepmother (it's a wonderful story), Florence Siegel-Lotker. I am also blessed with three wonderful and loving children: Howie (now married to Sodja), Stefanie, and Andrea. They are a credit to their mom, Carol, who worked so hard to take care of us all. We are a family who is there for one another in every time of and every kind of need and joy. I am proud to be a part of them.

And my love and thanks to Sonia Chriqui-Banon, who provided direction to my life, my career, and this book. Her intelligence, her insight, her instinctive wisdom, her sense of gratitude for life's gifts, and her inner and outer beauty inspire all who know her.

1
Introduction

PERSONAL INTRODUCTIONS

I'd like to thank you for investing your money and, more important, your time, in acquiring and reading this book. I'd also like to introduce myself. I'm a serious Jew in my mid-fifties and have held a wide variety of professional positions. Trained as a physicist, I have spent most of my career working with both U.S. and Israeli companies on alternative energy development. Some time ago, I gave up all this to devote myself to Jewish studies and interfaith activities and begin five years of full-time studies in order to become ordained as a rabbi. I am currently the rabbi for Temple Ner Ami in Camarillo, California, a suburb of Los Angeles.

My passionate interest in Judaism as an adult was stimulated by my search to understand and respond to my wife's tragic illness (Huntington's Disease). Although I had received a perfunctory Jewish education as a child, I never realized that my religion could provide me with such comfort and direction and my life with such significant meaning until tragedy struck my family. So, for the past twenty years or so I have been studying, taking classes, teaching classes, and leading services at my synagogue. I had been certified as a rabbinic aide by the Union of American Hebrew Congregations prior to becoming a full-time rabbinic student. I have also led services and taught classes at "student pulpits" in Arizona, southern California, and western Montana. In addition, I have been studying Christianity and Islam and have increasingly engaged in dialogue with people of good will from these religions. I have taught in Catholic schools and spoken to a wide variety of Christian groups. I believe that the Jewish mission in the world, to heal the world and solve our world's problems (Hebrew *tikkun olam*), is complemented by these two great monotheistic faiths. I further believe that we are at a time of unequaled possibility for dialogue and understanding among the religions. That's why I've written this book.

Who are you? In writing this book, I assume that you are a Christian who takes Christianity seriously. Most likely, you have come in contact with Jews at work or in your social life. Perhaps you and your children have Jewish friends, Jewish dates, or even Jewish spouses; perhaps you have Jewish in-laws, grandchildren, or other relatives. Perhaps you take your Hebrew Bible seriously (Jews prefer this term to *Old Testament,* since the latter implies acceptance of the New Testament) and want to learn more about the religion of Jesus.

So I'll assume that you're curious about Judaism and that you are motivated to understand and appreciate rather than to judge and condemn. My guess is that you know something about Judaism but that you're a bit shy about asking some of the most troubling and most important questions. Why don't Jews accept Jesus as the Messiah and Lord? Why do Jews have special dietary laws? Why are Jews so attached to Israel—aren't Jews Americans first? Perhaps the Jews you've asked don't know the answers to your questions. Or, even worse, your Jewish friends "know" the answers they've heard at their dinner tables from parents and relatives who didn't really understand these complex issues.

PURPOSES OF THIS BOOK

Let's be clear about what this book is and is not.

1. **It Is Designed to Be an Easy-to-Use Guide:** It is not a scholarly treatise documenting the essential elements of Judaism or comparing Judaism to Christianity. If you're in need of a more complete discussion of Judaism, you should consult some of the texts cited in the Bibliography. In fact, I hope this book will motivate you to pursue your Jewish studies further.

2. **It Is an Introduction to Christianity's Jewish Roots:** Most Christian theologians would acknowledge that one cannot truly understand Christianity without understanding the

Judaism of Jesus. I hope to help you do this as well as to enable you to further understand the development of Judaism since the time of Jesus.

3. **It Is a Compendium of Asked and Unasked Questions:** If Judaism is important to you, you will have lots of good questions to ask. You deserve authoritative and straightforward answers. You may be reluctant to ask such questions because the Jewish people in your life may be close friends or family whom you do not wish to offend. Maybe, when you have asked these questions of different Jews, you got different answers (consistent with the old joke that if you have two Jews, you have three opinions). Here's help.

4. **It Is an Introduction Focused on Christian Concerns:** There are lots of wonderful books on Judaism; this one focuses on questions important from a Christian perspective.

5. **It Is an Invitation to Dialogue:** It is my prayer that, after reading this book, you will join in dialogue with fellow Christians and Jews about the commonalities and differences between our two paths to God. This text can enhance such discussions. I hope that somewhere, someone is writing the Christian complement to this book so that we Jews can better understand Christianity as well.

6. **It Is Not a Conversion Tract:** It is not my intent to weaken your faith in Christianity or to convert you to Judaism. It is not my intent to resolve the theological differences between the two religions or to write *the* exhaustive treatment addressing every conceivable question that you may have about Judaism. This is an appetizer designed to stimulate your interest. *Bon appetit!*

A WORD ABOUT USING THIS BOOK

My goal is to give you the information that you need when you need it. Don't think that you have to read through the entire book in the order presented. Burning with curiosity as to why Jews don't accept Jesus as Messiah? Jump directly to chapter 4. Headed to a *Bar Mitzvah* this weekend and want to know what to expect? Chapter 8 is for you. Do your eyes glaze over when the subject is history? Feel free to skip chapter 3 with my blessings (although I hope you'll come back to it someday). I've tried to write each chapter as a self-contained unit; this means that there may be some overlap and repetition. But please, browse, thumb, skip through the book. Enjoy!

WHY IT'S SO IMPORTANT
TO UNDERSTAND EACH OTHER

Although there have been some bright spots, Jewish-Christian relations over the past two thousand years have been characterized by hate, distrust, and misunderstanding. The Holocaust has vividly shown where antisemitism[1] leads. Today, we find ourselves in a society where members of our two religions live side by side. On a worldwide scale, many Christian churches are increasingly recognizing and seeking forgiveness for their historic antisemitic teachings. Jews, living among Christians, are discovering that Christians are not all Jew-haters, that they are warm, loving, good people whom our children are dating and marrying.

At a price too high to be worth it, indeed too high to be imagined, the Holocaust has ushered in an historic challenge and opportunity for Christians and Jews to bury our theological hatchets and learn to live together in peace. Important statements have been issued by groups of Jewish and Christian scholars in this regard (they are included as appendixes to this book). Who knows how long this window for understanding may remain open? If we don't take advantage of it in our generation, to what may we be condemning future generations?

My friends, I believe that this is a window in time when you and I must talk together, study together, and pray together. Those of you with children know the special joy felt when we see our children support each other, help each other, and love each other. That our children have different personalities, different beliefs, different ways of living their lives diminishes our pride not one iota. We are all children of the one living God. Our time may be *the* time of the long-awaited family reunion. Consider this your invitation!

---

1. Chapter 6 explains why I've chosen this spelling of antisemitism.

2
Judaism: The Basics

You probably know Jews who say, "Yes, I'm Jewish, but I'm not at all religious. In fact, I don't believe in God. You might say I'm a cultural Jew."

What should we make of this? Can someone be Jewish but not agree with any of the major beliefs of Judaism? Can someone be a cultural Jew just because he likes bagels and lox and hot pastrami? Does this mean someone can be a cultural Methodist or a cultural Catholic? What's going on here?

ON THE NATURE OF JUDAISM

As nationally syndicated radio talk show host Dennis Prager likes to say, there are only two groups who often misunderstand the nature of Judaism: Jews and non-Jews. Among the world's cultures and religions, Judaism is unique in being both a religion and a people. Judaism is a *religion* in that it teaches a set of religious beliefs and practices, and anyone can enter Judaism by conversion. Jews are also a *people* in that entry into Judaism is most commonly by birth, and continued membership exists irrespective of one's beliefs. Let's look at this more closely.

The Jewish Religion: The idea that Judaism is simply a religion like Lutheranism, Catholicism, or Islam is relatively recent. Until the Enlightenment in Europe in the eighteenth century, both Jews and non-Jews largely understood Judaism to be a culture and Jews to be a people apart from other peoples. In fact, it was not until after the French Revolution that Jews began to be accepted as citizens of

European countries[2] (although Jews did have a legal, albeit sub-servient place in Christian society from medieval times). After that time, it became attractive to hold that Judaism was simply one of the world's "normal" religions, that there was nothing different about Jews other than their religious beliefs, that Jew-hatred was simply another form of religious intolerance, and, perhaps most important, that Jews could stop being Jewish by simply changing their religious convictions. (In the history of antisemitism, only the Nazis held that Jews could never stop being Jewish; see chapter 6 for a more complete discussion.)

To many Christians, this view makes excellent sense. Jews are simply holders of different theological beliefs, and do not recognize Jesus as Lord and Messiah. If Christianity is a religion that one can enter and exit by virtue of one's beliefs, so too must be Judaism. After all, if one can become a Jew after a course of religious instruction, rituals, and declarations of faith, he ought to be able to leave the Jewish people (or so many Christians and Jews incorrectly believe) by abandoning these religious beliefs.

Judaism is indeed a religion with distinguishing beliefs, rituals, clergy, liturgy, and scripture. This aspect of Judaism is not a matter of confusion. What is confusing and often misunderstood is that Jews are also a people.

The Jewish People: As my teacher, Rabbi David Wolpe suggests, if the word weren't so loaded with cultural overtones, it might be best to describe the Jewish people as a tribe. As is the case with membership in a Native American tribe, an individual is born into the Jewish people and remains a Jew for life (in the eyes of Jewish law) irrespective of his or her beliefs. If one joins the "tribe" through the religious act of conversion, one also becomes a Jew for life. From its earliest beginnings, Judaism has thought of itself as a nation and a people, as well as a guardian of unique religious beliefs.

Traditional Rabbinic Judaism holds that one's Judaism is passed from mother to child, that is, a child is considered Jewish if its mother is Jewish, irrespective of its father's religion. As a result, a child of a Jewish father and a non-Jewish mother is not considered Jewish. In Judaism, there are no "half Jews" or "quarter Jews"; you are either

---

2. Paul J. Kirsch, *We Christians and Jews,* Fortress Press, 1975, p. 113.

fully Jewish or not Jewish at all. This rule of matrilineal descent probably arose as the result of the experience of Jews being raped and/or sent into captivity; one cannot always be sure of the father of a child, but one knows its mother with certainty. It has also been observed that since a child spends most of its early years with its mother, this parent is likely to have the major impact on religious development and identity. It's interesting to note that in biblical times, one's tribe (of the twelve biblical tribes) and religion (and other matters of inheritance) flowed through the father's line; the change to matrilineal descent occurred in postbiblical times.

More recently, the Reform and Reconstructionist movements within Judaism have allowed for patrilineal descent, provided that the child is raised Jewishly. This has led to great controversy revolving around the validity of changing the laws of descent; the controversy does not involve the nature of the Jewish people. All the movements would agree that Jews are members of a people and that Judaism is far more than a religion.

In practice, this means that if one is born a Jew, one is a Jew irrespective of one's beliefs about God. Thus, the atheist child of a Jewish mother would be considered by Judaism to be as Jewish as the chief rabbi of Jerusalem, subject (in theory at least) to all of the requirements of Jewish law such as keeping kosher, praying regularly, and so on. Clearly, such a person would not consider himself bound by Jewish traditions and obligations and might well not consider himself Jewish at all or might call himself a "cultural" Jew. If he decided to become Jewishly observant, no conversion ceremony or process would be required.

If a Jew were to convert to another religion and reject Judaism, she would still be considered Jewish for purposes of her obligations to Jewish law but would not be eligible for any of the privileges of Judaism such as being called to read or bless the Torah. The child of such an apostate woman would be considered fully Jewish even if born after the woman converted out of Judaism.[3] Similarly, the child of a woman who converted *to* Judaism is considered fully Jewish provided that the child is born after the conversion.

---

3. *Encyclopaedia Judaica,* article on *Apostasy,* Keter Publishing House Jerusalem Ltd., 1972, vol. 3, p. 211.

Thus Jews are considered members of both a religion and a people. Jews have specific obligations concerning fellow Jews that transcend country of origin, race, or ethnicity. Although Jewish law provides that one should be loyal to one's country and obey its laws, this holds only so long as there is no conflict with Jewish law and obligations to God. Once someone converts and becomes a Jew, fellow Jews are forbidden to remind the person of her non-Jewish roots; the convert is fully Jewish in the eyes of Jewish law, as if from birth.

THE THREE PILLARS OF JUDAISM

Judaism, irrespective of the particular movement, may be said to rest on three "pillars" or fundamental elements: God, Torah, and Israel. While the various movements may emphasize one of these aspects above the others, no movement that has ignored any aspect has long survived.

God: A central prayer in Judaism, the *Shema,* declares that "the Lord is our God" and "the Lord is One." Jews believe in one God who is personal, powerful, present, just, and loving. We believe that God created humankind in His[4] image and, as a result, human life and dignity are sacred. The fact that there is one God means that there is one standard of ethical behavior for everyone as well as one integrated universe and one integrated humanity. Since Judaism is not a dogmatic religion, there is no specific set of principles, creed, or "confession" about God (or anything else for that matter) that Jews must believe. But at the center of Judaism is God, who must be addressed.

Jewish tradition assigns many names and titles to God, including *Elohim* (God), *El Shaddai* (God Almighty or the God of the Mountain), *Adonai* (this word means "my Lord" and is said when the unpronounceable name of God, YHVH,[5] is written in the biblical text or prayerbook), *Ha Maqom* (the Place), the King (or Master) of the Universe, the Merciful One, the Omnipotent, the Omnipresent, among

---

4. From time to time, I will use the personal pronoun *His* or *Him* to refer to God. Judaism does not, of course, hold that God is male, but I do think that the euphemisms for God that one tries to use to avoid reference to gender are often more distracting than helpful.

5. Written as the Hebrew letters *yod, hey, vov,* and *hey.*

others. While all of the references to God mentioned here and all the references in the Hebrew Bible refer to God in the male gender, rabbinic writing and mystical traditions also speak of the *Shechina,* or the Presence of God, in feminine terms. Judaism does not hold that God is male or female or corporeal in any sense, but understands that we are limited to using finite human language to discuss the Infinite One. Similarly, when the Bible speaks of the hand of God or God being jealous or angry, we understand it to be applying human characteristics as a metaphor through which to understand God.

Judaism understands God to be a Creator, a Revealer, and a Redeemer. Modern Jews understand the stories of creation to be emphasizing *who* created the universe and not *how* it was created. While there have been books written to reconcile scientific and biblical stories of creation,[6] most Jews would focus on the principal teachings of the first chapters of the book of Genesis: that we all come from the same source and that our mission is to complete the work of creation. (Although it is tempting to address scientific and historical conflicts in the book of Genesis, I believe this misses the point.) We also understand God to be a revealing God; it is not enough for God to have created the universe and humankind, He also seeks to communicate His love for us and His specific requirements of us through the Bible and other sacred Jewish texts. Finally, God is our Redeemer. God has set a direction to history, a direction of growth from slavery to freedom, from ignorance to education, and from disease to health. God cares about His creation and has acted in history and will be a continuing force in our future. Our primary mission as Jews is *tikkun olam*—to heal and repair the world. In assigning us this mission, God has made us a true partner in completing creation.

The God Jews worship is the same God Christians worship (and for that matter, the same God Muslims worship). This makes our dialogue-encounter different in nature from other interreligious relationships. Jews do not accept the Christian concept of the Trinity, however. Similarly, the idea of God taking on corporeal human form, as an incarnation through Jesus, is inconsistent with the Jewish conception of God. On the other side of the coin, some Christians assume Jews worship only the *Father* of the Trinity, which is held to be the Lord of Justice, in contrast with the *Son,* as Lord of Mercy and Love.

---

6. G. L. Schroeder, *Genesis and the Big Bang,* Bantam, 1990.

These Christians make the mistake of concluding that the God Jews worship has little love and mercy. For Jews, God is the source of both justice and mercy.

Torah: The Hebrew word *Torah* means "instruction" but holds a wide variety of meanings for Jews. At the narrowest, it refers to the handwritten scroll found in synagogues containing the first five books of the Bible. The word also refers to these books in their printed form and, more broadly, to both the written Torah (the five books) and the oral Torah (the Mishna and Talmud — see pp. 22–24 for a fuller explanation of these terms). Beyond this, the word *Torah* refers to all of Jewish sacred literature, including the extensive commentaries on the Bible and Talmud. In a still broader sense, Torah can be used to represent one's own teaching. For example, I would hope it would be said of me that my Torah is one that will bring Jews and Christians to a better understanding and appreciation of the principles and beauties of both religions.

Including Torah as one of the three pillars of Judaism means to emphasize the importance of revelation to Jews. I often speak of two major leaps of faith in religion. The first (and for me, the easiest) leap of faith is belief in God. The second leap contains the assumption that this source of order and intelligence in the universe would care enough to take the time, trouble, and effort to reveal His wishes and instructions for humankind. I think it's easier for most of us to believe in God than to believe that the Torah and Bible (and, by extension, other sacred texts) are the result of God's desire to communicate with us. However, pursuit of religion means adopting a faith in terms of its revealed scriptures. Therefore, I live with a faith that the God that ordered the stars in the heavens and set the laws of physics and mathematics in place cares how I treat my neighbor and even cares about what I eat for lunch!

When Jews study the Bible and other sacred literature, we probe for deeper and hidden meanings. Our tradition holds that there are at least four levels of meaning in the Torah's verses, from the simple to the mystically hidden. We study texts printed with the commentaries of the rabbis living in our own time and those living thousands of years ago. We read the text as we might the words of a letter from a lover who can only communicate once in a very great while. Each word is precious and each is scrutinized. Why is this phrase stated in this particular way? Why is there an odd spelling here or an enlarged letter there? Each and every "jot and tittle" in the text is analyzed and discussed. In one form of analysis, the numerical value of words (each Hebrew letter represents a number) is used to pry hidden meanings from the text. Rabbi Lawrence Kushner encourages us to look at the text as the collective dream of the Jewish people. If you had a dream that you were being chased by an enemy and the sea parted to let you through but crashed in on your pursuers, you would not analyze the physics of the miracle but why it happened and what it means to you and your deeper consciousness. This is how we approach Torah.

Torah study is at the height of Jewish practice. In one Talmudic formulation that has become a part of the daily liturgy, we are taught that the study of Torah is equal to a long list of deeds of extraordinary merit because such study leads to them all. Most synagogues have Torah study classes on Saturday mornings during which students study the biblical portion of the week or some other topic of Jewish interest. Often non-Jews will be welcome at such sessions and will find new depths of understanding in the Hebrew Bible. Ideally, the Torah should be studied in its original Hebrew so that the full riches contained can shine through. For example, in Hebrew, the connection between human being *(adam)* and earth *(adamah)* is apparent (the human having been formed from the earth). Knowing the language of the Bible helps us realize that the name *Israel* means to struggle with God. Many students would, in fact, equate Torah study with the wrestling or struggling with God.

Torah study is a lifetime's work with infinite breadth (including as it does Torah, Bible, Talmud, codes, *responsa,* etc.) and infinite depth. I have on my bookshelf an entire book devoted to the word *echad* (meaning "One") as used in the *Shema* prayer. For me, the Torah is like a river and its study is like a journey of exploration down the river. The river is there and flowing all the time. We can only spend so much time in the river and only explore a tiny portion of it. We choose to explore some sections in much greater detail than others. We may linger in a particular little cove for a moment or for the rest of our lives. The joy is in knowing how beautiful the river is, in the physical and intellectual comfort that comes from immersing yourself in the river and the reassurance of knowing that it is always there. There is no hint that our job is to master or complete the study but only to continue it and to participate in it.

An important Jewish concept is that direct revelation from God was completed with the scripture that we have. One fascinating story in the Talmud (*Bava Metzia* 59b) relates that during an argument among several rabbis over a question of Jewish law, one rabbi called upon successive physical miracles to support his position, which had been rejected by the majority. The fact that he caused a tree to walk, a stream to run backward, and walls to cave in did not impress the others. When at last the voice of God Himself spoke on his behalf, the other rabbis, in effect, told God to "mind Your own business: that the interpretation of scripture is 'not in heaven.'"[7] The Talmud relates that God's reaction was to laugh and exclaim that "my children have bested me," much as any proud parent would upon realizing that her child is a capable, responsible adult. The point is that the Jew's role with respect to Torah and revelation is not passive. We are expected to struggle with and study the text and make it meaningful in our lives and times. Tradition holds that any new interpretation of the text that we might realize was originally given to Moses on Sinai and it has taken us this long to rediscover it.

Israel: Jews have spoken of the *people* Israel and of the *land* of Israel since biblical days, even though the modern *State* of Israel has only existed since 1948. Clearly we mean something much broader. In the Bible, the Jewish people are often called *b'nai Yisrael,* or the children of Israel. This refers to the renaming of the third and final patriarch, Jacob, whose name is changed to Israel after he wrestles with what is generally understood to be an angel (Gen 32). We believe that God has chosen the people Israel for the task of taking the message of God's supremacy and ethics to the world. In the covenant that God makes with Israel, God promises the survival of the people and nation of Israel in the so-called Promised Land so long as we keep our side of the bargain and comply with God's Torah. Tradition holds that all Jews ever born or ever to be converted into Judaism were present at Sinai when this convenant was enacted.

The Jewish attachment to the land that is modern-day Israel dates back to these biblical promises to the first Jew, Abraham, and his successors. The land is promised to us only so long as we treat it and its inhabitants according to God's law. The Talmud teaches that

---

7. Quoting Deuteronomy 30:12.

we were expelled from the land and from our Temple because of our acts of injustice. Although the majority of Jews have lived outside the land since the original expulsion in 586 B.C.E., there has never been an independent state in the land other than a Jewish state. Traditional Jews pray for the ingathering of Jews back to the land daily, and they pray for rain during the time when it is needed in the land of Israel. Many of the 613 commandments can only be fulfilled in the land. Simply put, Judaism is a religion and people inextricably associated with what is today the land of the State of Israel.

Similarly, each Jew feels attached to every other Jew in the world since we are all part of one people. Thus, when Jews in the former Soviet Union or Ethiopia are in need, Jews around the world will come to their aid. The Law of Return of the State of Israel provides that any Jew has automatic citizenship as an Israeli and therefore needs no naturalization process. Jews are a people that transcend borders and races and cultural categorizations. In a sense, the State of Israel is the ultimate melting pot, with Jews of some 130 nations coming together to fulfill the provisions of the covenant.

3
Judaism: Much More Than the Religion of the Hebrew Bible

When I mentioned that I was thinking of writing a book for Christians about Judaism, a Christian friend of mine responded saying, "You know, if we only studied our Old Testament more diligently, we would know a lot more about Judaism." It was exactly this kind of misconception that convinced me that this book was needed. The study of the Hebrew Bible[8] will no more give you a complete picture of modern Judaism than would the study of the Christian Bible give a Jew an understanding of modern Christianity.[9] The religion Jews practice around the world today may be more accurately described as the religion of the Talmud and the rabbinic tradition than as the religion of the Hebrew Bible.

In this chapter, I give my perspective on how Modern or Rabbinic Judaism and Christianity developed out of the roots of the Hebrew Bible and how a body of sacred Jewish literature developed in the postbiblical world. Please understand that this perspective is both oversimplified and personal. I am not a scholar in this field; please refer to the bibliography for more scholarly presentations. What follows is how I have come to make sense of what is, for many, a difficult and confusing area.

I begin with an historical discussion of how Jews and Christians responded to the events of the first century with the creation of our

---

8. I will use the term *Hebrew Bible* rather than *Old Testament* since the use of the latter term implies that the Hebrew Bible is incomplete or replaced, a belief inconsistent with Judaism. Some Jews find the term *Old Testament* offensive.

9. For example, where in the Christian Bible would I find an explanation of the differences between Protestant and Roman Catholic Christianity?

distinct sacred texts. This is followed by a discussion of central Jewish texts beyond the Hebrew Bible and how the various Jewish movements may be understood as distinctive responses to these texts.

THE HEBREW BIBLE: THE ROOT OF AND ROUTE TO TWO TRADITIONS

The relationship between Christianity and the Hebrew Bible may be well known to you. Jesus and his earliest followers in Palestine were Jews who lived for the most part in accord with the commandments and laws of the Hebrew Bible. They believed Jesus to be the Jewish Messiah prophesied in the Bible. Christians came to understand Jesus to be the fulfillment of the Hebrew Bible and its laws as a whole and not just simply of the passages on the Messiah, so that while Christians respect and revere the Hebrew Bible, they do not see themselves to be bound by many of its rules such as those relating to dietary laws, wearing ritual garments, observance of the Sabbath on Saturday, and so on. Most Christians assume that Judaism is simply the religion that continued to live by the rules and regulations of the Hebrew Bible. This is more than an oversimplification; it is simply not true!

You may be surprised to learn that Modern Judaism, like Christianity, is a religion that finds its roots in the Hebrew Bible (or Written Torah), which it sees as part of a greater whole that requires completion by the inclusion of rabbinic literature (or Oral Torah). The Christian Bible was a response to a singular event in the Christian world (the birth, death, and resurrection of Jesus, understood to be the Messiah and God incarnate). While traditional Jews believe that the Oral Torah was revealed at the same time as the Written Torah, many scholars understand part of rabbinic literature as a response to the destruction of the Holy Temple in 586 B.C.E.[10] and again in 70 C.E.[11] We might think of the Christian Bible and rabbinic literature as two branches growing from a single tree trunk,

---

10. Jews, like modern archaeologists, use the terms C.E. (Common Era) and B.C.E. (Before the Common Era) instead of the terms A.D. (*Anno Domino:* in the year of our Lord) and B.C. (Before Christ).

11. Although rabbinic literature begins well before the destruction of the Temple, it assumes unquestioned dominance only after this event.

that of the Hebrew Bible. Both Christianity and Rabbinic Judaism were responses to momentous events that required a new understanding of Hebrew scripture.

Momentous Events and Responses

Christianity: The Arrival of the Messiah: The most significant event in the history of the world for Christians is the life, death, and resurrection of Jesus. In Christians' eyes, Jesus came to solve a singular problem in a singular way. The problem was original sin (the fundamental sin that alienated all humans from God) and humanity's inability to fulfill God's law completely and perfectly. (As discussed later in this book, these were not problems for the rabbis and Judaism.) The means of atonement for original sin was explained in terms taken straight from the Hebrew Bible and from the Jewish practice of the day, namely, sacrifice. For the most encompassing of all sins, Christianity understands that the most perfect of all sacrifices, the sacrifice of the sinless son of God, who took on our human nature to atone for all our sins, was necessary. With his resurrection, Jesus was revealed as the Christ (Christ is a Greek translation of the Hebrew word *mashiach*, which means "the anointed one"; much more on this in chapter 4).

Judaism: The Destruction of the Temple: The event that ultimately transformed Biblical Judaism into Rabbinic Judaism was the destruction of the Holy Temple in Jerusalem in 70 C.E. As the first half of the book of Leviticus makes clear, the primary means for the biblical Jew to relate to God was through sacrifice, especially animal sacrifice. While the early Jews would set up altars for sacrifice in several locations, the book of Deuteronomy (12:5–6) tells us that we could only offer sacrifices at "the site that the Lord your God will choose." This site was to become the Holy Temple in Jerusalem.[12] The destruction of the First Temple in 586 B.C.E. raised for the first time the issue of how Jews could relate to God without a Temple and without sacrifice. The rebuilding of the Temple some seventy years later made this problem a temporary one. The final

---

12. Or had already become the Temple. Biblical scholars believe that the book of Deuteronomy was probably written during the reign of King Josiah in the latter part of the seventh century B.C.E. (see W. Gunther Plaut, *The Torah, A Modern Commentary,* Union of American Hebrew Congregations, 1981, p. 1291).

destruction of the Second Temple in 70 C.E., and the failure of the Bar Kochba revolt (see below) in 135 C.E., made the problem permanent.

During the period beginning with the destruction of the Second Temple, and ending four hundred to five hundred years later, the rabbis restructured Judaism. They took a tradition based in animal sacrifice and transformed it into one based in prayer. They took a religion closely tied to a sacred land and a sacred location, and transformed it into one capable of surviving in exile (although, as we have seen in chapter 2, still strongly tied to the land), one that Jews could take with them throughout the world. This was accomplished through laws and customs contained in the rabbinic literature. Remember, all of this took place after the time described in the Hebrew Bible. Thus, a Christian or Jew attempting to understand Judaism by reading the Hebrew Bible alone would be unaware of these changes.

In the same time period that the founders of Christianity were writing the Christian Bible, the rabbis of Judaism were completing the compilation of the Mishna, the first tier of the two-tiered Talmud. The two works were in formation during the same period; each reflected an understanding of Hebrew scripture in the context and aftermath of the momentous events of the first century C.E.[13]

In the same way that Christianity may be said to be the religion of the Christian Bible, Modern Judaism may be characterized as the religion of the Talmud. Today, if you were to follow an observant Jew throughout his or her day and year and question the origin of the many distinctively Jewish practices that fill the Jew's world, you would learn that they are predominantly traceable to the Talmud. The laws and traditions that Jews observe originated to some extent in the Bible itself but have all been filtered through the lens of the Talmud. Even those holidays mentioned in the Bible, such as Passover and the High Holy Days (see chapter 7), have been interpreted in the Mishna, Talmud, and Midrash (these terms are more fully explained below) and have had the details of observance defined in these texts.

---

13. Stephen M. Wylen, *Settings of Silver,* Paulist Press, 1989, p. 181.

JEWISH HISTORY FROM THE TIME OF JESUS
TO THE COMPLETION OF THE TALMUD

To understand the transformation of Judaism from Biblical to Rabbinic, we must briefly review some of the history of this transformation. Let's look at each of the critical time frames briefly.[14]

Judaism around the Time of Jesus (50 B.C.E.–50 C.E.): During this period, the major Jewish population centers were in the land of Israel, then a province of Rome, as well as in Babylon and Egypt. Jews in the land of Israel and in Babylon spoke Aramaic, the already established language of international trade and diplomacy, while Jews in Hellenistic Egypt spoke Greek and relied on a Greek translation of the Hebrew Bible called the Septuagint (translated c. 250 B.C.E.). The name *Septuagint* (from the Greek word meaning seventy) comes from the tradition holding that each of the seventy scholars charged to translate the Bible came up with the exact same translation, proof of the divine inspiration of their work.

In 37 B.C.E., the Romans appointed Herod king of Judea. Although unpopular, Herod was the great builder who brought the already existing Second Temple to a state of grandeur never before achieved. After his death in 4 C.E., a series of procurators (including Pontius Pilate) were installed by Rome, placing Judea under Rome's direct control. During these troubled times there were at least five major sects of Jews:

- The *Sadducees,* the upper class and priestly party, were proponents of the status quo. They recognized only the Written Torah and Bible and rejected the concept of the Oral Law (explained below). Since this group was tied to the Temple and Temple-based worship, they disappeared after the destruction of the Temple.
- The *Pharisees,* who represented the middle and lower classes, were the precursors of Rabbinic Judaism. They believed that an Oral Law was given to Moses on Mt. Sinai and that God

---

14. It is beyond the scope of this book to present a thorough review of Jewish history. An excellent and thorough presentation may be found in Wylen's *Settings of Silver, a*s well as in any number of books about Jewish history. See the bibliography for suggested reading.

could be worshiped with study and prayer in the absence of being able to sacrifice at the Holy Temple. The Pharisees developed the concept of the synagogue and religious courts and the role that these institutions were to play in Judaism. They introduced the academies that were to develop Rabbinic Judaism. Although Jesus condemned many of the Pharisees of his day in the Gospel accounts, and the name *Pharisee* became much maligned in Christian history (so much so that the dictionary definition of the term includes "sanctimonious, self-righteous or hypocritical person"[15]), some scholars believe that, based on his teachings, Jesus was a Pharisee.[16] Modern, Rabbinic Judaism sees itself as a successor to Pharisaic Judaism, holding that it was the Pharisees who were responsible for saving Judaism after the destruction of the Temple.

- The *Essenes,* a monastic sect, believed that the Temple leadership (and indeed all of society) had become corrupt. They lived in isolation from the main body of Jews in places like Qumran, where the Dead Sea Scrolls were found. They believed that God would soon bring the world to an end. It is likely that John the Baptist was an Essene.

- The *Zealots* were in favor of armed revolt against the Roman rulers. Rival armies within the Zealot camp fought against one another while the rebellion against Rome took place. They destroyed the food stocks in Jerusalem during the Roman siege of the city in order to inspire the citizens to fight. After the city was conquered, a group of Zealots escaped to the Herodian fortress of Masada, where they held out for more than two years before committing mass suicide rather than surrender to the Roman Legions and become slaves.

- The *Nazarenes,* as the early Christians were called (in fact, the modern Hebrew term for Christian is *Notzri*), were yet another Jewish sect of the time—a time of great turmoil and messianic expectations. As the history of Judaism and Christianity proves, the turmoil of the times was to usher in great innovations and changes in religious worldviews.

---

15. *The Random House Dictionary of the English Language,* Random House, 1973, p. 1079.

16. Karen Armstrong, *A History of God,* Ballantine Books, 1993, p. 81.

The Destruction of the Temple and the Bar Kochba Revolt (70–135 C.E.): Following the failed revolt against Rome and a three-year siege of Jerusalem, the Second Temple was destroyed on the ninth day of the Hebrew month of Av.[17] This was, of course, a major crisis and turning point for Judaism. How could a religion that was centered on the practice of offerings and sacrifice at the Holy Temple in Jerusalem survive without the Temple itself? Did the destruction of the Temple signify the powerlessness of Israel's God or even the error of worshiping this particular God? Was it now appropriate to worship the gods of the victors, the Roman gods? The decisions and steps taken by a small group of rabbis were to answer these questions and ensure the survival of Judaism.

During the siege of Jerusalem in 70 C.E., Rabbi Yohanan ben Zakkai escaped from the city by feigning death and leaving in a casket. Legend says that ben Zakkai succeeded in establishing a school and relocating the Sanhedrin (the governing body of Judaism) to the town of Yavne by predicting that the Roman general, Vespasian, would become emperor of Rome (thereby earning a favor from the new emperor). To this Sanhedrin fell the task of reformulating Judaism into a religion based on prayer and fulfillment of divine commandments, a radical change from its sacrificial roots. Judaism changed from a religion centered on Temple worship and rite to one centered on sacred acts, or *mitzvot,* and on a prayer-based relationship with God, practiced in the synagogue and home. The calendar of holidays was reinterpreted, and the emphasis on the agricultural nature of holidays was refocused onto historical origins.

The final revolt against Rome lasted from 132 to 135 C.E. and was led by Simon Bar Kochba. The rebellion may have been triggered by Roman attempts to forbid the teaching and practice of Judaism. The best known and most revered rabbi of the time, Rabbi Akiva, declared Bar Kochba to be the Messiah.[18] The revolt failed, however, and with it, Bar Kochba's claim to messiahship. More than 500,000

---

17. *Tisha b'Av,* the 9th of Av, is considered to be the date of the destruction of the first Temple in 586 B.C.E. and the date of the expulsion of Jews from England in 1290 and Spain in 1492. For these reasons, it is observed in Judaism as a day of fasting and mourning.

18. Some scholars speculate that this declaration led to the irreversible separation of Christianity and Judaism. Christianity could not remain as a Jewish movement if someone other than Jesus was recognized as Messiah.

Jews were killed, about half of Judea's population. Survivors were sold into slavery and forbidden to enter Jerusalem, and the Romans salted large parts of the land of Israel so that nothing could grow. The Sanhedrin was forced to relocate to Tiberias near the Sea of Galilee, where the task of continuing the development of Rabbinic Judaism was carried on.

Completion of the Mishna and Talmud (200–600 *c.e.):* Jewish tradition holds that Moses received two types of revelation on Mt. Sinai, the Written Torah and the Oral Torah. As its name suggests, the Oral Torah was meant to be sustained by transmission from one generation to another by word of mouth, perhaps to animate it to respond to each generation's needs while keeping it distinctly separate from the ultimate authority of the Written Torah. With the destruction of the Temple, the failure of the Bar Kochba revolt, and the subsequent expulsion of Jews from Jerusalem, there was a fear that if the Oral Torah were not written down, it might be lost forever. The force behind the writing down of the Oral Torah was Rabbi Judah the Patriarch (*Yehuda ha-Nasi*). His redaction became known as the Mishna (from the Hebrew verb, "to teach") and became the basis for the Talmud. "Rabbi," as he is simply known in rabbinic literature, assembled the Mishna in about 200 c.e. The academies that existed in the land of Israel and in Babylon continued the study and teaching of the Mishna and of Judaism.

The two academies continued their analysis of sacred Jewish literature, including the Mishna, over several hundred years. The laws and traditions of the Mishna were discussed to determine how they could be applied to build a structure of Jewish law (called *halacha*). In the fourth century, as Christianity became the state religion of the Roman Empire, the academy in the land of Israel was ordered closed by the authorities and the rabbis hurriedly composed the record of their discussions by following a written *mishna* with a discussion called a *gemara* (from the Aramaic word for "learning"). The combination of the Mishna and the Gemara is known as the Talmud. A separate Talmud was compiled in Babylon and in the land of Israel. Since the community in Babylon had about a hundred years longer to assemble its Talmud, and since the final assembly or redaction was accomplished under less stress, the Babylonian Talmud is far larger and considered more authoritative than the Talmud of the land of

Israel (also called the Jerusalem Talmud although it was actually composed in the Galilee region). The written Talmuds are regarded by traditional Jews as the Oral Torah, divinely revealed at Mt. Sinai, a major element of sacred literature. It is important to understand that the Talmud is not all legal material. There is also a wealth of folkloric material (called *aggadah*) as well as material that explains and amplifies the content and meaning of biblical passages (this material is called *midrash;* its preparation and compilation continued long after the Talmuds were redacted).

JEWISH SACRED LITERATURE BEYOND THE BIBLE

"Boy, I'd sure like to read the Talmud someday," a Jewish friend responded after I told her that Judaism is more correctly said to be the religion of the Talmud than of the Hebrew Bible. Many Jews and more non-Jews have no idea what the Talmud is. That's a shame because it is an interesting and engrossing library of material developed over many centuries. The Talmud is far too lengthy and difficult for an evening's (or even a year's) reading; it is traditionally the focus of a lifetime of study. It is an encyclopedic work designed not only to determine *halacha* or Jewish law on a particular matter, but to teach Jews how to reason and think so as to be able to continue developing Judaism and Jewish law in the centuries to come.

1. **Mishna:** Taken by itself, the Torah leaves many questions unanswered. For example, the Torah commands us to refrain from work on the Sabbath but tells us very little about what it considers work. Is feeding the children work? Is leading a prayer service work? Jews look to the Mishna to resolve such questions. Regarding work prohibited on the Sabbath, the Mishna identifies thirty-nine specific activities as work. These establish principles for determining whether some new activity that was never contemplated in antiquity (such as driving a car or riding in an elevator) should be considered work from the perspective of the Sabbath.

    The Mishna is divided into six sections called orders, which in turn are divided into sixty-three tractates. Individual citations (each one also called a *mishna*) are cited by tractate, chapter, and verse in a format similar to biblical citations. For example, to quote Rabbi Hillel in the *Pirke Avot* 1:14 (i.e., the fourteenth *mishna* in the first chapter of tractate *Pirke Avot*), "If I am not for myself who is for me? And being only for myself what am I? And if not now, when?" To give you a feel for the size of the Mishna, a standard translation into English[19] is almost 850 pages long, a bit smaller than an English translation of the Hebrew Bible.

In a very real sense, the Mishna is the response of the rabbis as to how to interpret the Hebrew Bible in the same way that the Christian Bible reflects that tradition's understanding regarding the same book. To cite but one example, Christian scriptures reinterpreted the Bible's "eye for an eye" requirement to stress mercy and turning the other cheek. The Mishna also reinterprets this same provision and provides a nonliteral reading. An "eye for an eye" does not mean that one who puts out another's eye is to have his own eye put out (suppose the offender has only one good eye; which one of his is to be removed?), but it means that just economic compensation must be made for the loss (medical costs, lost time, and other economic loss) and for the suffering of the victim.

2. **Gemara:** The Mishna provides the rabbis' theoretical world-view of Judaism, one adapted to the post-Temple world. For some two hundred to four hundred years following the completion of the Mishna, two main schools of rabbis discussed various *mishnayot* (the plural of *mishna*) leaving us the Gemara or the record of these discussions. In her wonderful introduction to the Talmud,[20] Rabbi Judith Abrams compares the Mishna to the Constitution of the United States: terse, orderly, logical, and changeable only with great difficulty. The Gemara corresponds to constitutional law as expounded by the federal courts and the Supreme Court. There is lots of detail, lots of case specifics, lots of interesting anecdotes, and often (but not always), a decision as to what the law will be. While the Constitution nominally has supreme authority, it has not gone unnoticed that the Constitution means what the

19. H. Danby, *The Mishnah,* Oxford University Press, 1933.

20. J. Z. Abrams, *The Talmud for Beginners; Volume 1 (Prayer),* Jason Aronson, 1993, p. xviii. *Volume 2 (Text)* and *Volume 3 (Living in a Non-Jewish World)* are also available from the same author and publisher.

Supreme Court says it means. In the same way, while the Torah and Mishna are the supreme, unchanging authorities, Jewish law is what the Gemara says these sources mean.

The combination of the Mishna and Gemara is the Talmud, which is divided into the same tractates as the Mishna (although not all tractates of Mishna have corresponding Gemara). In addition to these two documents, the pages of Talmud studied by Jews today have numerous other commentaries and discussions on the same page.

The Talmud reads like an ongoing set of discussions about the Mishna (perhaps a bit like the *Congressional Record*). The reader is drawn into arguments among rabbis who may be contemporaries or of different centuries; a fourth-century C.E. rabbi may be called upon to answer a question raised by a second-century C.E. rabbi about a first-century B.C.E. *mishna*. The discussion may range far and wide in a "stream of consciousness" way. The technique draws the student in, giving life to the text. The Talmud contains both legal *(halachic)* and nonlegal *(aggadic)* material, the latter including fascinating and amusing stories. Traditional Jews hold the study of Talmud to be the highest sort of scholarship. Such scholarship is invaluable since the Talmud text assumes that the reader is familiar with the entirety of the Talmud and all other sacred Jewish literature. These traditional Jews would hold that the basis for the solution to every human problem that has ever and will ever arise can be found in the pages of the Talmud (see the example below). Even liberal Jews, who may not see the Talmud as the literal word of God, recognize the crucial role the Talmud has played in shaping Modern Judaism.

Since 1523, the way in which a Talmud page is printed has been standardized. Figure 1 illustrates how such a page looks, with the *mishna* and *gemara* sections along with the major commentaries. Because of this standard printing, a talmudic citation is by tractate and page number; the reference *Bava Metzia* 12b refers to the backside ("b" page rather than the front or "a" side) of the twelfth page (or folio) of the tractate *Bava Metzia*. Unless otherwise specified, talmudic references are to the Babylonian Talmud rather than the much smaller Jerusalem Talmud.

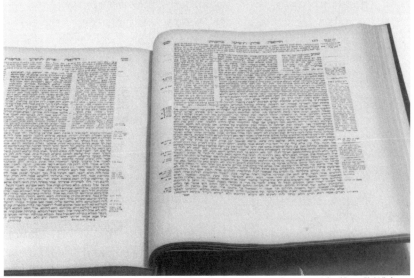

Figure 1: A Page of Talmud

TORAH AND *HALACHA:*
A MUCH BROADER CONCEPT THAN LAW

My teacher Rabbi Frank Rosenthal used to say that "every translation is an interpretation." When the Hebrew Bible was translated into the Greek Septuagint in the third century B.C.E., the Hebrew word *torah* was translated into the Greek as *nomos*. Nomos is understood to mean law (in a narrow legal sense) and torah is often translated as "law." Significantly, this translation captures only one element of the meaning of the Torah. As viewed by Jews, the Torah is far more than a book of laws. It is seen as the very blueprint for the universe, as a gift from God to humanity, as a vessel of love and guidance with which we are nurtured throughout our lives and throughout the centuries. According to some Christian theologies, Jesus had to die as a perfect sacrifice since Jews (not to mention the rest of humanity outside the covenant) could not hope to fulfill all the terms of the "law" and therefore all humans would live in a state of inescapable sin rooted in original sin. This interpretation misunderstands the Jewish perspective concerning God's view of sin and law. We believe that since God knows our nature, God understands that we cannot comply with each and every minute aspect of *torah* and Jewish law.

The Hebrew word for Jewish law, *halacha,* comes from the verb, "to walk." *Halacha* is understood by observant Jews to be God's directions to us as to how to live our lives in accordance with the plans of the Designer of life. The rules are not seen as difficult burdens to be bemoaned and removed, but lovingly given rules of life's game that make life more understandable and meaningful. You might compare it to the lines and net of a tennis court. Do tennis players long for a game that would remove the lines and net so that they would be free to play the game according to their personal styles and wishes? Of course not! Just as the rules of tennis give the game its very meaning, traditional Jews see *halacha* as giving meaning to the game of life. There is no thought or need for anyone or anything to remove what is not considered as a burden.

Halacha begins with the laws found in the Torah (the tradition holds that there are 613 *mitzvot,* or commandments, to be found in the Torah). In the example cited above, Exodus 20:10 tells us we should do no work on the Sabbath. The Mishna further specifies that work includes carrying objects and the Talmud continues the discussion by going into specific instances of permissible and forbidden forms of carrying. Much (but by no means all) of the Talmud is devoted to discussion of legal/religious issues with the objective of determining what is the proper *halacha* on the issue. Legal decisions are necessary about the aspects of day-to-day life. In Judaism, there is no dogma about such ideas as what specifically will happen to me when I die, but there must be a determination that will tell me whether (for example) this chicken is kosher. I don't need to know how many levels of heaven there are, but I do need to know if I can serve this bird for dinner! (Check the section of chapter 7 explaining kosher foods to learn more.)

Codes: Since Jewish law is dispersed throughout the many volumes of the Talmud, the task of determining the *halacha* on a given issue could prove quite daunting. Since many questions of law arise again and again in Jewish communities, a number of codes of law were developed to assist rabbis in their legal decisions. The two best known of these are the *Mishne Torah* (meaning "a second Torah"), compiled by Moses ben Maimon (or Maimonides) in the twelfth century, and the sixteenth-century *Shulkhan Arukh* of Joseph Karo. The latter is still regarded by Orthodox Jews as the standard legal code. In it, the Jew finds detailed instructions on virtually every aspect of day-to-day living.

Responsa *Literature:* Of course, the codes of law cannot address every question that will arise. Beginning almost immediately after the completion of the Talmud, questions concerning actual problems of living were submitted to *halachic* authorities. The answers to these questions, called *responsa* (singular, *responsum*), were collected into volumes and became part of Jewish law. These *responsa* would address how situations never contemplated in the Talmud or in subsequent codes should be handled. The authors would go back to scripture and the Talmud for insights and principles. Often, a Talmudic principle developed for one reason would be used to resolve a very different problem.

My favorite example of this process lies in the resolution of the question as to whether artificial insemination (using sperm other than the husband's) is to be considered adultery and whether the resulting child is illegitimate under Jewish law. In reaching a decision on this question, the rabbis cite a curious portion of the Talmud that examines whether the High Priest, who could only marry a virgin (according to Lev 21:13), would be able to marry a virgin who had given birth. The case considered is one in which a virgin in a public bath may have conceived by coming into contact with a seminal emission from a man in the same bath. The Talmud (*Hagigah* 15a) concludes that the woman would, for purposes of her eligibility to marry the High Priest, still be considered a virgin. Well over a thousand years later, the authorities debating the legitimacy of artificial insemination could conclude that, based on Talmudic principles, the procedure did not constitute adultery.[21] Traditional Jews see this as an example of God having planted the answer to a humanly unforeseeable question in the Talmud.

Response to* Halacha: *Orthodox, Conservative, Reform, and Reconstructionist Movements: As detailed in chapter 7, one of the major differences in the various Jewish movements is their response to *halacha:*

- Orthodox Jews believe that Jewish law derives from the Oral and Written Torah, the literal word of God given to Moses on Mt. Sinai, and is therefore binding on their lives and that the laws revealed in scripture, Talmud, and the classic codes are

---

21. Joel Sirkes (1561–1640) in *Bach* to *Tur, Yoreh De-a* 195 cited in *American Reform Responsa*, #157 *Artificial Insemination*, CCAR Press, pp. 500–501.

Image copyright of SweetChild Software

Figure 2: Traditional Jewish Headcoverings
(Hebrew: *kippah*; Yiddish: *yarmulke*)

unchanging although the laws may have to be adapted to new situations.

- Conservative Jews accept Jewish law as binding but they believe that *halacha* can and must change as the times change. Thus, Conservative Jews are able to drive on the Sabbath and have synagogue seating in which men and women sit together.
- Reform and Reconstructionist Jews do not hold the entire body of Jewish law to be binding but generally accept the ethical laws as binding. They leave it to the individual Jew to accept or reject ritual laws, such as the kosher laws and those relating to ritual dress (*kippot* and *tallit,* or head-coverings and prayer shawls, for example). The concept of giving Jewish law a "vote but not a veto" is often heard in this context.

In practice, the degree to which individual Jews observe *halacha* will vary greatly, even within a movement. Some Jews keep kosher in their homes but not when dining out. Still others will restrict their restaurant menus to vegetables or fish and avoid eating meat while out of the home. Increasingly, some Reform Jews will adopt elements of *halachic* observance such as dietary laws or wearing a *kippah* (see figure 2). Even among Orthodox Jews, there will be disagreements concerning details of observance in areas as basic as the fitness of various kinds of milk and as abstract as the legality of the use of certain cosmetics on Passover.

* * *

Judaism has not been frozen in time for the past two thousand years. It has been growing and developing and responding to the challenges that arrive in every age. Christians should understand that the Judaism of their friends and neighbors is not the Judaism that existed in the time of Jesus. Judaism today is much more than the religion of the Hebrew Bible.

4

It's More About *What* Is the Messiah Than *Who* Is the Messiah

"It all seems so easy. You are waiting for the Messiah; we think he's already come in the person of Jesus. Why can't you just accept that he's come and go on being Jewish? What's the big deal?"

The above is the substance of a discussion I once had with a "Jew for Jesus." "Jews for Jesus," often called "Messianic Jews" or "Hebrew Christians" (there are several separate organizations), adopt a tantalizingly simple approach. "We are Jews," they say, "who believe that the Messiah has come and it was indeed Jesus whom we accept as Lord and Savior. In all other ways, we're Jewish." As you might guess from the title of this chapter, there's more to the difference between Judaism and Christianity than the single question: "Was Jesus the Jewish Messiah?" The heart of the matter concerns (1) who was—who is—and/or who will be the Messiah but, in my opinion more important, (2) what is the Messiah and, by extension, who and what is God.

SIGNIFICANCE OF THE MESSIAH IN JUDAISM AND CHRISTIANITY

You may be surprised to learn that when Jews and Christians say the word *Messiah,* they mean very different things. The concept of Messiah is very important to Judaism, but is by no means central. A teaching of Rabbi Yohanan ben Zakkai (the leader of the Jewish people after the destruction of the Temple in 70 C.E.) captures this very well: "If you are planting a tree and you hear that the Messiah has come, first finish planting the tree, then go to greet him."[22] The lessons are many. There have been and will be many people claiming to be the Messiah. If this one's real, you'll know soon enough. And just as important, the things you do in this world for your community and children to build a better world (symbolized by planting the tree) are of greater importance than immediately greeting the Messiah.

The Jewish Concept of the Messiah: The Hebrew word for messiah is *mashiach,* literally meaning "anointed one." In biblical times, the ascension of kings to their positions was marked not with a crown but with holy oil being poured over their heads, *anointing* them. The Hebrew Bible describes many men as *mashiach,* including Jewish priests (Lev 4:3), prophets (Isa 61:1), kings (1 Kings 1:39), and even Cyrus of Persia, a non-Jewish king (Isa 45:1). The Greek translation of the Hebrew *mashiach* is *cristos,* from which the English word *Christ* comes. When speaking of Jesus, as a Jew, I try to be careful to refer to him as "Jesus" and never as "Jesus Christ" or "Christ." To refer to him as "Christ" would be to describe him (through two layers of translation) as Messiah.

Very little is written directly about the Messiah in the Hebrew Bible (in fact, the title "the Messiah" as a specific personality does not appear at all), although there is considerable discussion in the Talmud, Midrash, and other rabbinic sources. While there is not absolute agreement on the details of the Messiah, virtually all Jewish sources would agree on the following points:

1. The Messiah will be *fully human and only human*. He will be born and die in the natural manner expected of any man. He will be a "son of God" in the same way each and every one of us is a "child of God." He will come from the line of King David.[23]

2. He will be a ruler (probably political and possibly military in the model of King David) and an agent of God who will

---

22. *Avot d'R. Nattan* (The Fathers According to Rabbi Nathan) 31, quoted in Wylen, *Settings of Silver,* op. cit., p. 99.

23. There is some discussion of a messianic figure of the priestly line (i.e., from the line of Aaron, Moses' brother, of the tribe of Levi) which, while apparently important to the Dead Sea Sect, has not figured prominently in Rabbinic Judaism. In addition, there are some references to a Messiah who would be a descendant of Joseph and would be a precursor to the arrival of the Messiah of the line of David.

restore the sovereignty of the Jewish people and usher in the Messianic Age, gathering the Jewish people from exile to the holy land (Isa 27:12–13 and Isa 11:12).

3. The Messianic Age will be a time of peace among all peoples ("they shall beat their swords into plowshares and their spears into pruning hooks," Isa 2:4) and even among animals ("the wolf shall dwell with the lamb," Isa 11:6). It will be a time when the entire world accepts the one God ("the earth shall be full of the knowledge of the Lord," Isa 11:9).

4. The Messiah will not be God. Only God is God and "God is One" (Deut 6:4). For Jews, the concept of God becoming human or taking on human form is foreign. There is no concept of anything resembling the Trinity of Christianity.

5. The Messiah will not be involved in the redemption of sin any more than any human Jewish leader, certainly not by his sacrifice. Only God is described as "Redeemer" in Judaism. Specifically, the Messiah will not come to redeem original sin since Judaism does not believe in original sin. For Jews, the salvation of the world does not depend on the Messiah but upon people doing the will of God as expressed in God's commandments.

Reform Jews have for the most part drawn away from the idea of an individual Messiah. They hold that the goal of Judaism (and of humanity) is to usher in a "Messianic Age" in which the prophecies concerning peace and redemption will take place. Even in traditional sources, there is great disagreement as to what the Messiah will actually do. The ideas range from the mystical, granting him fantastic powers in the tradition of biblical prophets, to the beautiful idea that the Messiah will come one day after he is no longer needed—after we humans have solved the world's problems ourselves. But nowhere is it suggested that the Messiah is other than human.

The concept of Messiah is not the central concept of Judaism. As a serious, committed Jew, the only time I have spent any time focusing on the Messiah as a reality is in dialogue with Christians. I have never attended a single adult study course or lecture focusing on the Messiah, although I suspect that I could have searched one or more out. As an illustration of this point, I checked my copy of the 16-volume *Encyclopaedia Judaica*. The article on *Messiah* covers 10 pages.

Compare this with a 25-page article on *Marriage,* a 27-page article on *Moses Maimonides* (a medieval Jewish philosopher), and a 40-page article on *Moses*. Messiah is not the central issue for Judaism that it is for Christianity.

There have been many people who claimed to be (or had followers who claimed they were) the Messiah in Jewish history, the most notable being Bar Kochba (leader of the final Jewish revolt against Rome in 135 C.E.) and Shabbetai Zvi (who attracted hundreds of thousands of followers in 1666). Jesus is the only such claimant who has had a significant impact well beyond his death. The lack of centrality of the Messiah to Jewish thought is illustrated by the fact that Rabbi Akiba, the leading rabbi of his time, was not discredited by his claim that Bar Kochba was the Messiah.

The Christian Concept of the Messiah: Any Christian reading the above will recognize the differences between the Jewish and Christian concepts of Messiah. The early church fathers developed the concept of Messiah into something beautiful and powerful, but something well beyond the Jewish concept described above. As most readers will know, the Christian Messiah, Jesus Christ, is held to be God and savior, a part of the Holy Trinity.

Historical Notes: As chapter 3 discusses, Christianity began as a small Jewish movement after the death of Jesus. Jews of that age largely rejected the Messiahship of Jesus since he did not fulfill the prophecies concerning peace and Jewish political autonomy. No ancient Hebrew text of the Christian Bible has been preserved, although it has been translated into Hebrew in modern times. Not even the success of Christianity in its outreach to the gentiles of the age, nor its adoption by the Roman Empire as a state religion convinced Jews of its teachings. That the conversion of Paul to Christianity was the result of an epiphany, a mystical revelation, underlines the powerful faith element of Christianity.

As a Jew who respects and admires Christianity, I am proud that my tradition gave birth to this beautiful religion. The idea that God would become a human Messiah and suffer all of the pains and sorrows of humanity, and even die a horrible death for the sins of humanity, is majestic, powerful, and moving. It is an idea that has resulted in an enormous amount of good in the world, a huge body of *mitzvot,* to use Jewish terminology. People have been clothed and fed and educated in its name. My country, the United States, was created by those moved by its teachings. One can argue that the Christian concept of Messiah has had a far greater impact on the world than the Jewish concept ever did, and I would not disagree. I simply do not recognize in this the Jewish concept of Messiah.

As beautifully put by Joseph Klausner,[24] "Without the Jewish Messiah, Judaism is defective, without the Christian Messiah, Christianity doesn't exist at all."

WHY DON'T JEWS ACCEPT JESUS AS MESSIAH?

You can now probably answer this question as well as I. Judaism does not accept Jesus as the Jewish Messiah because Jews do not believe that he fulfilled the basic prophecies concerning the Messiah. Specifically, he did not bring about world peace or draw the entire world to the worship of the one true God. He did not return the Jewish exiles to the Holy Land,[25] bring an end to idolatry, or end famine. Of course, Christianity would respond that these prophecies will be fulfilled with Jesus' second coming.

Christians read the Hebrew Bible from a different perspective that discovers how Jesus did indeed fulfill Jewish prophecies concerning Messiah. It is not the purpose of this book to refute those citations in detail for two important reasons. First, I have no desire to reduce Christians' faith in their religion. My prayer is that Christians become more faithful and religious. Moreover, for those interested, the work has already been done in both a short pamphlet form[26] and a more scholarly, book-length treatment.[27]

Jews and Christians read the Hebrew Bible differently. Jews do not accept the premise that the Hebrew Bible is understandable only through the eyes of the Christian Bible, a concept clearly articulated

---

24. Joseph Klausner, "The Jewish and Christian Messiah," in *Disputation and Dialogue,* KTAV Publishing House, 1975, p. 68.

25. An interesting sidebar to this point is that there are certain ultra-orthodox groups in Israel today who do not recognize the State of Israel since it was not founded by the Messiah.

26. Rabbi Bentzion Kravitz, *The Jewish Response to Missionaries,* Toronto, 1996.

27. Gerald Sigal, *The Jew and the Christian Missionary: A Jewish Response to Missionary Christianity,* KTAV Publishing House, 1981.

by Saint Augustine's dictum that "in the Old Testament, the New Testament lies hid; in the New Testament, the Old Testament becomes clear."[28] I can understand Christian interpretations of the Hebrew Bible as intellectually and historically important, but Jews cannot accept such interpretations as the primary meaning of the sacred scripture.

As a final note on this subject, I want to correct a mistaken impression that many Jews and Christians have: that Judaism, while not accepting Jesus as Messiah, nevertheless accepts him as a prophet.[29] This is not true. For Judaism, prophecy closed with the last Hebrew prophet, Malachi. It's natural and understandable that religions close prophecy in order to exclude prophets who come after the closure of their sacred scripture. Jews no more accept Jesus as a prophet than do Christians accept Muhammad (the great prophet of Islam) or Christians or Muslims accept Buddha or Joseph Smith (prophet and founder of The Church of Jesus Christ of Latter-day Saints faith).

It should now be clear to you why Jews have such a problem with "Jews for Jesus" or other presentations of Messianic Judaism. I have no difficulty with Christianity. I even accept those Christians who would want me to convert to Christianity so long as they don't use coercion or duplicity and are willing to listen in good faith to my reasons for being Jewish. I do have a major problem with those Christians who would try to mislead me and other Jews into believing that one can be both Jewish and Christian. It is no more meaningful to be an authentic *Jew for Jesus* than it would be to be a *Christian for Muhammad* or a *Muslim for Buddha*. The teachings of Christianity, beautiful as they are, are simply as inconsistent with Judaism as the teachings of Islam are inconsistent with Christianity. One could have been a Jew for Jesus in the first century C.E., but not since then. I believe that the "Messianic Jewish" organizations seek to seduce Jews into believing that they can remain Jewish while accepting Jesus. The crucial question that should be asked of such Messianic Jews is the very simple question "Is Jesus God?" As Judaism and Christianity define themselves, no Jew can answer this question in the affirmative and no Christian in the negative.

---

28. Quoted by Mary C. Boys in "Typology in the Catechism of the Catholic Church," *Catechism of the Catholic Church — Catholic and Jewish Readings*, Anti-Defamation League Interfaith Focus, vol. 1, no. 2, 1994.

29. It is noteworthy that Islam does indeed treat Jesus as a prophet.

5
Judaism and Christianity — The Important Similarities and Critical Differences

We now understand why Jews don't accept Jesus as Messiah and what Jews mean when we say "Messiah." But this is not the end of the story. Christianity is much more than Judaism plus a messiah and Judaism is much more than Christianity minus Jesus. This chapter explores what our traditions share as well as where they differ.

THE SIMILARITIES

Before we dive into the many differences between Judaism and Christianity, let us acknowledge the commonalities that underlie the two religions. By focusing on what we share, we can sharpen our appreciation for the ways in which the two traditions have taken the basic truths revealed by God and transformed them into two separate living faiths.

On the Nature of God: Our most important commonality is, of course, our deity. We worship the same God, who is also worshiped by the world's billion Muslims. We all worship the God of Abraham whom we believe to be Creator, Revealer, and Redeemer. We believe that this God has given us, through our sacred texts, a combination of inspiration, instruction, and commandments that teach us what He wants of us. Our traditions teach us that this God is transcendent but also immanent, omnipresent, infinite, eternal, unchanging, omnipotent, creative, omniscient, merciful, compassionate, holy, sovereign, good, and just (to name just a few adjectives).[30] We see ourselves in a relationship with God who has created us not just to serve Him but to care for His creation. We believe that this relationship, or covenant, has obligations on both sides.

That we hold God to be a God of justice is a critical point. We do not see God the way the Greeks saw their gods, as often playful characters perpetrating tricks and schemes on helpless humans who would turn to bribery to influence them. That God is just moves Abraham to challenge Him to live up to His own standards regarding the destruction of Sodom and Gomorrah. "Shall not the Judge of all the earth deal justly?" Abraham asks in Genesis 18:25. When we ask "where was God at Auschwitz?" or "why were so many killed in this earthquake?" or "why was my innocent child taken from me?" and other questions of this nature, we make the implicit assumption that God is a just and good God. If this were not so, we would have no basis upon which to question God's actions in the world.

We also hold that God is a God of justice and mercy. Both of our traditions stress that God's desire is not to punish the sinner but that the sinner turn from sin and repent. Since mercy is considered to be especially characteristic of the Christian concept of Jesus, that he is ever-forgiving and ever-compassionate and ever-loving, some Christians conclude that the justice-seeking aspect of God must reside in the "Father" element of the Trinity. Since many associate this element with the "God of the Old Testament/Jews," they mistakenly conclude that the Jewish view of God is of a God who is primarily concerned with vengeance and punishment. This is not the Jewish view of God, as can be seen in the way the High Holy Day prayerbook addresses God: "This is Your glory: You are slow to anger, ready to forgive. Lord, it is not the death of sinners You seek, but that they should turn from their ways and live. Until the last day You wait for them, welcoming them as soon as they turn to You."[31]

Our Common Scripture: Once again, this simple point needs to be underlined. We share a common sacred text, which Jews call the *Tanach* (see glossary) and Christians call the Old Testament.

---

30. Various denominations and movements will differ on the specific nature of God, each having its own approach to theology. I describe here the areas of general agreement in broad terms.

31. *Gates of Repentance,* Central Conference of American Rabbis, 1984, p. 314.

Christianity's adoption of the Hebrew Bible is the result of a conscious choice by the early church fathers in the second century in disavowing the movement of the heretic Marcion to reject the authority of the Hebrew scriptures.[32]

Our common scriptures give us the basis for improved dialogue and understanding. Some of the most wonderful experiences I have shared with Christians both in the United States and in Jerusalem have been in connection with study of these texts and how our two traditions have come to understand them. Fascinating issues of translation and interpretation arise which, in my experience, lead to a better mutual understanding. Beyond this, when we gather together in prayer, we may have the pleasure of praying from the same texts, whether it be from Psalms, Proverbs, the book of Job or the Ten Commandments. That we each derive separate lessons and diverse inspiration from these texts is testament to their power and universality.

Although we read the same scriptures in the Hebrew Bible, there are a few differences worth mentioning. The Christian order of the books of the Bible is not the same as that found in the Hebrew Bible. The Catholic Bible includes a number of books (the Apocrypha) in its "Old Testament" that are not included in the Hebrew and Protestant Bibles. There is also a particular way that a Jew studies text—with the commentaries and analyses of others. It is almost unthinkable that a Jewish study of the Bible would not include the opinions and insights from rabbis and experts of the Talmudic and medieval periods alongside the text. While this approach is shared in Catholic tradition, it certainly differs from the *sola scriptura* ("scripture alone") approach that is more typical among Protestants.

Our Common Ethics: This is a point that I don't think is stressed enough. Both of our traditions teach what has become known as the Golden Rule: the Jewish version being stated in the negative as "What is hateful to you, do not do to your fellow man,"[33] and the Christian version being stated in the positive as "Do unto others as you would have them do unto you."[34] While there are those who would focus on the different motivations of Jews and Christians in their conduct of ethical behav-

---

32. Walter Harrelson and Randall M. Falk, *Jews and Christians: A Troubled Family,* Abingdon Press, 1990, p. 20.

33. Quoted in the Babylonian Talmud, tractate *Shabbat,* p. 31a.

34. Matthew 7:12.

ior—those who would stress that Jews are following specific details of Jewish law while Christians are imitating Jesus, we should focus on the actual practice. The bottom line for a Jew is that good works, acts of lovingkindness, of mercy, of charity, included in what we Jews would call *mitzvot,* are done in the world. A hungry person cares less about the motivation of the supporters of the food bank than he does about the availability of nourishment for his family. So do we—and so does God.

Our Common Hope for a Redeemed World: This is another point that is so obvious that it is easy to overlook. Judaism introduced, and Christianity adopted, the idea of redemption. While I will address the differences in the way we see redemption below, both traditions see the world moving from historic and present days of problems to a future world that is better, even perfect. Both traditions stress the idea that we are to work to make peace, cure disease, govern fairly, and improve the lot of humankind. Both traditions believe that history has direction, that we are not intended to live within a repeating cycle of slavery, despair, hunger, war, and disease. And in both traditions, we find religious people hard at work to improve the world even though they may be motivated by very different theologies.

Prayer: Once again, it seems so obvious that we might overlook it. Both of our religions turn to communicate (to address and to listen) with God through prayer. In both traditions, prayer consists of both formal liturgy spoken in sacred assembly and in the words and meditations of the heart spoken silently or aloud, within a group or alone. We believe that God listens to and answers prayer, even if sometimes the answer is "no."

THE DIFFERENCES

Although they began from a common root, Judaism and Christianity parted ways almost two thousand years ago. It is not surprising that they have developed into very different traditions. While recognizing that the different approaches that the many Christian denominations and various Jewish movements take makes generalizations risky, let's examine the major areas of Jewish-Christian difference.

Faith versus Works: While Judaism certainly does not ignore issues of faith and Christianity does not ignore good works, it is appropriate to say that Judaism emphasizes the role of right actions over right thought while Christianity stresses faith over deeds. Judaism has no official creed or statement of faith that is used in ceremonies of maturity (*Bar* and *Bat Mitzvah*) or in conversion.[35] Since the vast majority of Jews are Jews by virtue of birth, there is no specific set of beliefs or dogmas to which we must ascribe. When a rabbi is ordained, he or she takes no vows. The focus in our tradition is on the performance of *mitzvot,* meaning commandments (and not simply "good deeds," as many believe) that God has given us. We believe that our obedience to these commandments is the primary desire of God. The Talmud quotes God as saying that "better that they (the Jews) abandon me, but follow My laws." (The Talmud adds that such observance will bring the Jews back to faith in God.)[36] Although the different Jewish movements take different perspectives with respect to the details of Jewish law and *mitzvot,* all would agree that it is our actions in the world, and not our private beliefs, that are of primary importance to God.

This is, of course, to be contrasted with the Christian perspective on faith and works. While Christian scripture acknowledges that "faith of itself, if it does not have works, is dead" (Jas 2:17), it stresses that right faith in God and Jesus as savior is primary. Christian history is replete with Church Councils that have set forth the specific creeds of belief to which adherents must hold. Failure to follow such creeds could result in a charge of heresy. When the belief systems of specific groups of Christians have varied significantly, it has often resulted in another new denomination. For Christians, the act of faith in Jesus as savior and redeemer is key; salvation depends on God's grace and mercy. In Judaism, the focus is on human adherence to divine commandments *(mitzvot).*

Meaning of Sin: The word *sin* is an example of a term that both Jews and Christians use to mean very different things. Although there are differences by denomination, when Christians use the word *sin,* they refer either to a state of being in sin or to actual sins people

---

35. There is a creed of sorts, Maimonides' Thirteen Principles, which appears in the liturgy but is not used in the same way Christian creeds are used.

36. Jerusalem Talmud, *Haggigah* 1:7.

commit. The first sense is especially apparent when they speak of "original sin" (the act of Adam and Eve in eating the forbidden fruit in the Garden of Eden) or being in "a state of sin." In this sense, Christians use the word sin first to mean the power of evil over a wounded human nature that needs divine grace to counteract it. Humans have won the full grace of salvation from the effects of original sin by the death of Jesus for all people. Christians receive this saving grace through Baptism. Thereafter, they speak of being in "a state of sin" only for people who do not seek God's forgiveness for their actual sins.

For Jews, sin is not a state of being but an action in contradiction to God's commandments. One Hebrew word for sin, *chet* (it rhymes with *late*), illustrates this very well. The word is a term from archery meaning "to miss the mark." God gives us the clear target for our behavior, a target that we may miss. People are neither fundamentally good nor evil but have both the inclination to do good (the *yetzer tov*) and the inclination to do evil (the *yetzer ha-ra*) battling within them. Sin is an action whose response demands repentance and forgiveness (see below). Perhaps a saying sums this up well: "In Christianity, man sins because he is a sinner; in Judaism, man is a sinner because he sins."

Original Sin and the Nature of Evil: Simply put, the disobedience (as the biblical text describes it) of Adam and Eve in the Garden of Eden is not the problem for Judaism that it is for Christianity and is not considered by Judaism to be "original sin." Our daily morning liturgy puts the Jewish perspective very clearly: "My God, the soul you have given me is pure." Our souls are not "stained" by the actions of Adam and Eve. While the Eden story is indeed part of our Torah and Bible, we do not draw the same conclusions and implications from the text. Even in biblical times, there was no Temple sacrifice that addressed original sin nor did any of the prophets refer to it. Thus, if we are to understand Christianity's interpretation of the life, death, and resurrection of Jesus as a response and solution to the problem of original sin, it is easy to understand why Jews do not accept this faith. For Jews, Christianity is a solution to a biblical problem that simply does not exist.

How does Judaism address the presence of evil in the world? As noted above, we believe that people are not born either fundamentally good or evil but have both natures within them. We understand that God is responsible for creating both good and evil in the world. As stated in the words of Isaiah 45:7, "(I am the One) Who forms light and creates darkness; Who makes peace and creates evil; I am the Lord, Maker of all of these." God is the author of everything in the world. Traditional Jews, upon hearing especially bad news such as the death of a loved one, recite the blessing: "Blessed are You, Lord, Our God, King of the universe, the true Judge." God has given us free will; people have the freedom to do good or evil, to build hospitals to preserve life or death camps to extinguish it. But when we go astray, we don't blame Adam or Satan; we have no one to blame but ourselves and only we, with God's help, can work toward our own repentance.

Repentance and Forgiveness: The Jewish concept of repentance (Hebrew *teshuvah*) is built around the idea of turning or returning. We repent for sins by first acknowledging and regretting the sin, next by confessing the sin, and finally by resolving not to repeat the sin in the future. For sins against other people (theft, insult, injury, etc.), one must first restore the damage done to the other person and request forgiveness from the other person before divine forgiveness is possible. We believe that God cannot forgive sins committed against other people until the sinner has sought and received forgiveness from the victim. Of course this requirement makes murder an inherently unforgivable sin. This does not mean that the murderer is irreconcilably condemned to eternal punishment. We Jews believe that God will judge our sins against our good deeds with compassion and mercy as well as with justice. We do not presume to know how any individual will fare. God alone has the power to forgive sins against God alone (blasphemy, ritual violations, dietary violations, etc.). As described in more detail in chapter 7, the most sacred and sober day of the Jewish calendar, *Yom Kippur* (the Day of Atonement), is dedicated to repentance.

For Christians, forgiveness of sin, whether original sin or specific violations, is an act of divine grace, an undeserved gift from Jesus/God. Christians are assured of God's willingness to forgive sins such as murder that would not be forgivable in Judaism. The key Jewish act of seeking forgiveness of the victim of the sin is not the precondition to divine forgiveness in Christianity that it is in Judaism.

Redemption and Salvation: Although Judaism believes in an afterlife, it is a religion that focuses primarily on *this* life. This is particularly apparent with respect to redemption and salvation. Judaism understands these to be primarily aspects of individual and communal life in this world. An individual Jew pursues redemption in this world by performing *mitzvot* in fulfillment of God's commandments. So too does the Jewish people achieve communal redemption and salvation by complying with God's laws. In this way, salvation becomes almost political in nature. Judaism holds that we humans have been given a divine role in God's plan for completing and perfecting the creation of the world. With the coming of the Messianic Age, personal, national, and universal salvation will merge in a world free of war and suffering.

If for Christians, the Messiah has already come, where is salvation? As I understand it the answer is twofold: first, Jesus will come a second time to fulfill the prophecies concerning world peace and so on, and second, salvation and redemption are to be understood as more personal, relating to one's soul in the world of life after death. For the Jew, redemption is something that all of us work on, with God's help, in this world even though it may be achieved long after our own time. In the words of the Mishna: "You are not required to complete the work, but neither are you at liberty to abstain from it."[37]

The Afterlife: Judaism, while holding that there is certainly a life after this one, has little to say about the specifics of that world. Once again, in Judaism the stress is on how one lives this life rather than on what the next one is all about. Even as God has entrusted us to care for this world, we trust that God will take care of us in the next. Although the Hebrew Bible itself has little to say about the afterlife, rabbinic literature has much comment and speculation but no authoritative descriptions. There are rabbis who focused on the immortality of the soul and others who believed in reincarnation. Traditional Judaism holds that physical resurrection of the dead will take place in "the end of days," but this is not a belief shared by the Reform movement. The afterlife is theologically necessary since we believe that God is good and just, and it is clear that goodness and sin are not completely rewarded and punished in this world. The Jewish view, however, offers few details with regard to reward and punishment in the "world to come."

---

37. *Pirke Avot* 2:21.

Spirituality and Materialism: A serious treatment of Jewish and Christian spirituality is well beyond the scope of this brief discussion; the goal here is to highlight the primary differences in approach. Jewish spirituality is rooted in scripture and prayer; the principal mystical text of Judaism, the *Zohar,* is structured as a commentary on the Torah. In contrast, Christian spirituality is focused on relationship with Jesus and imitation of his life and ways. Another major difference between Jewish and Christian spirituality is the tendency of the Christian approach to distinguish between the body of flesh and blood on the one hand, and the spirit on the other. This is an echo of the Greek philosophy that so influenced the original Christians. Plato's idea that "the soul is the prisoner of the body" led some Christians to believe that they had to war against their flesh to save their souls.[38] By contrast, mainstream Judaism does not treat the spiritual as the antithesis of the material; as a Jewish maxim states, "body and soul are like friends and lovers to each other."[39] As Abraham J. Heschel notes: "The Hebrew bible is not a book about heaven—it is a book about the earth."[40] Judaism, with its focus on the *mitzvot* to be performed in this world, largely rejected an overly ascetic approach to spirituality, such as monasticism. While a Jew might be tempted to go off for years to commune with God, doing so would make performance of the *mitzvot* of having a family, giving to charity, and caring for the needy (to name just a few) impossible.

* * *

This chapter has only touched on what I believe to be the most important and interesting similarities and differences between Judaism and Christianity. Interested readers are referred to an excellent book[41] devoted entirely to exploring Jewish and Christian perspectives on these as well as twenty-eight other interesting subjects.

---

38. Peter Stravinskas, article on Spirituality in *A Dictionary of the Jewish-Christian Dialogue,* L. Klenicki and G. Wigoder, Editors, Paulist Press, 1995, p. 198.

39. Abraham J. Heschel, "Israel: An Echo of Eternity," *Disputation and Dialogue: Readings in the Jewish-Christian Encounter,* Frank E. Talmage, Editor, KTAV Publishing House, 1975, p. 193.

40. Ibid., p. 194.

41. *A Dictionary of the Jewish-Christian Dialogue,* op. cit.

6
Antisemitism

I have, thank God, spent far more time reading, writing, and speaking about antisemitism than I have experiencing it. Once when I was about ten or so, a "friend" called me a "dirty Jew." No big problem; it was handled by my Mom speaking to his Mom. About eight years later, I engaged a young man, who had called my younger brother the same epithet, in a fist fight (my one and only actual fist fight to date). That's it. That's my total personal experience with anti-Jewish hatred directed against me and my children. Although I've worn a *kippah,* or skullcap, identifying me as a Jew for the world to see over the past seven years and have never tried to hide my Judaism, I have not knowingly been the target of antisemitism. So what's the big deal here? Why are Jews so "obsessed" with anti-semitism, or Jew-hatred?

As we will see, antisemitism is a part of Jewish history and a part of every Jew's consciousness. It shaped our religion and has shaped our lives. One week ago today, as I was gathering my notes and material for the first draft of this chapter, a white supremacist opened fire on a Los Angeles area Jewish Community Center, firing seventy rounds of automatic fire at kindergarten-age Jewish children. He was later quoted as telling the FBI that he considered his deed to be "a wake-up call to America to kill Jews." A few days later, swastikas were spray-painted on the walls of an area synagogue along with the words "Jews die." Several weeks earlier, three synagogues in Sacramento, California, were fire-bombed. At about the same time, a gunman shot at eight Jewish worshipers just outside a Chicago area synagogue.

You cannot fully understand Jews and Judaism without understanding antisemitism, that unique form of hatred we Jews have experienced for more than two thousand years. Virtually every country that has had a significant Jewish community (with the important exception of the Americas) has expelled its Jews at some time during its history. I know of no Jewish family whose history has not been dramatically affected by antisemitism. My own grandmother left Russia about a hundred years ago to escape Russian pogroms (organized, government-sponsored anti-Jewish riots). Traveling on her own at age fifteen, she came to New York City to join her brother who had preceded her. Other Jews I know fled Germany in the 1930s and Morocco in the 1960s. Ask your Jewish friends how they or their ancestors came to America and you will have your own glimpse of how antisemitism changed personal histories.

We will explore some of the historical, theological, and psychological reasons for Jew-hatred. While I will do my best to make this subject understandable, I confess that much of it is simply beyond my comprehension. It is one thing to discuss theology, it's quite another to understand why ordinary Germans, raised by their parents to be good and honorable members of society, volunteered for duty that included burning babies alive.

UNDERSTANDING ANTISEMITISM

Talk to five people and you will get ten or more explanations for antisemitism. They will tell you Jews have been hated because they are rich, powerful, stubborn, and snobbish (although poor, weak, cooperative, and friendly Jews have not escaped), that Jews have been the target of racism (although there are Jews of every race), that Jews have been used as scapegoats, or even that Jews are guilty of having murdered God (some two thousand years ago). If you read the article on antisemitism in *Encyclopaedia Judaica*,[42] you will find a lengthy discussion (seventy-four pages with numerous illustrations—and this does not include the seventy-eight-page article on the Holocaust itself) of antisemitism as it has manifested itself over the past 2,500 years. But why? Why?

In philosophy there is a concept known as Ockham's razor—which says that one should not assume the existence of more things

42. *Encylopaedia Judaica,* op. cit., vol. 3, pp. 87–160.

than are logically necessary to explain a concept. In this spirit, I find the explanation of antisemitism by Prager and Telushkin in their book, *Why the Jews: The Reason for Antisemitism,*[43] compelling. They explain that it is only in the last century that we find antisemitism so puzzling. Before this, Jews have always understood Jew-hatred as a consequence of their Judaism. Antisemitism is a response to Jewish beliefs, teachings, and peoplehood. This explains the fact that, with the single exception of Nazi genocide, in every age Jews could escape persecution by simply joining the majority culture and forsaking their Jewishness. Prager and Telushkin's book and thinking have helped me to understand antisemitism and to write this chapter. In fact, I adopt their suggested spelling of *antisemitism* rather than the more common anti-Semitism, which suggests that there is a concept, Semitism, that anti-Semitism opposes. I recommend their work to you.

As discussed in chapter 2, Judaism rests on three main elements: God (or Jewish faith and belief), Torah (or Jewish law and custom), and Israel (or Jewish peoplehood). Let's look at the ways in which antisemitism is a response to each of these central Jewish elements.

God: It may sound strange to think of it in these terms but one could argue that Jews were the first religiously intolerant people. Before Judaism, pagans seem to have tolerated worship of other gods. In prebiblical and biblical times, if you visited another land, you would worship the gods of that land alongside or instead of your own. Judaism, on the other hand, had the chutzpah to say that there is only *one* God, *our* God (an invisible one at that!), and that all other gods were false.

Later on, Christians opposed Jews and Judaism for their refusal to accept Jesus as messiah and God. Muslims could not forgive Jews for refusing to accept Muhammad's prophecy and revelation as true. Nazis and Communists could not tolerate the Jewish idea that there is only one source of ethics and values, which was not the *Führer,* not the Party, not even the popular vote of the people. The idea that Jews have been *chosen* by God for a particular mission, an idea that is historically central to Judaism, has led to antisemitism as well.

Torah or Jewish Law: There are several elements of Jewish law that have resulted in antisemitism. *Kashrut,* or the Jewish dietary laws,

---

43. D. Prager and J. Telushkin, *Why the Jews: The Reason for Antisemitism,* Simon and Schuster, 1983.

make it difficult if not impossible for religiously observant Jews to eat with non-Jews. Similarly, observance of the Sabbath has served to keep the Jews separate from the larger world in both ancient and modern times. However, in requiring that Jews live and proclaim Jewish teachings in this world, Jewish law denies Jews the option of living like the Amish of Pennsylvania in their own world, maintaining only a minimum necessary contact with the larger society. Furthermore, the fact that Jews continued to live by Jewish law was a public demonstration of their denial of Christianity and Islam and their teachings. In addition, Jewish requirements regarding education, study, and learning meant that large numbers of Jews were literate and often successful. Observance of Jewish traditions regarding family, community, charity, and abhorrence of violence have also served to make many non-Jews jealous of the benefits of these teachings. Jewish tradition meant that Jews had to do more than simply cling to a different set of beliefs, they had to translate these beliefs into the way they live in an often hostile world.

Israel or Jewish Peoplehood: As discussed more fully in chapter 2, Judaism has always defined itself as both a religion and a people or nation. This was true even before 1948, when the *State* of Israel was created. Even though I am not a citizen of the State of Israel, I am a member of the nation or people of Israel. This is one of the most perplexing aspects of Judaism for non-Jews (and even some Jews) to understand. Zionism is the historical attempt to translate this traditional national element of Judaism into an actual political entity, the State of Israel. At the present time, most antisemitism is focused on this national element of Judaism.

Since the Enlightenment, it has been common for Jews to hear: "Just behave as any other religion. Keep your beliefs private. Are you loyal to France (for example) or to the Jewish nation? Abandon your national aspirations and you'll be accepted." Thus, modern Jew-hatred can be disguised as anti-Zionism. Today, the antisemitism of the Left and of Islam is often directed at the State of Israel and at Zionism. But this is simply a subterfuge; one cannot be pro-Jewish and anti-Israel any more than one can claim to be a lover of the French people and simultaneously call for the destruction of France. This is especially true since the destruction of the State of Israel would almost certainly require the death of the almost five million Jews living there as well as the other Jews of the world who would hasten to their defense.

A word about "dual loyalty" is in order. Prager and Telushkin explain this very well.[44] Although I am a member of two nations, the United States and Israel, I am only a citizen of one (the United States). My loyalty is to one government alone. Further, under Jewish law, I am obligated to obey the laws of the nation of my residence so long as its laws are not immoral. Thus, I obey speed limits, civil law, and criminal law. If a law were passed that was immoral or required me to violate some aspect of Jewish law (such as a law requiring Christian prayer), I would be duty-bound to resist it. To date, such a conflict has never arisen in my life and I pray it never will.[45]

THE HISTORY OF ANTISEMITISM

Although many Jews think that antisemitism is primarily a Christian or Muslim creation, as we will see, it predated both religions and has been present in those who consider themselves enemies of all religions, namely, Nazis and Communists. What follows is the briefest of presentations of a complex and intricate subject. Entire libraries have been written on the subject of Nazi antisemitism alone. I refer you to the bibliography for further reading.

Antisemitism in the Ancient World: The earliest record of Jew-hatred may be found in the Hebrew Bible itself. The book of Exodus, in describing the birth of Moses, reports that the Egyptian pharaoh decreed the death of all Jewish baby boys as part of a master genocidal plan. The biblical book of Esther tells the story of an attempt to destroy all the Jews of Persia in the fifth century B.C.E. Later on, during Hellenistic and Roman times, Jews were unique in refusing to worship the gods of these dominant cultures and, as a result, subject to antisemitism. The holiday of Hanukkah celebrates one such episode in which Antiochus Epiphanes attempted to destroy Judaism in 167 B.C.E. (despite his and other Hellenistic rulers' tolerance for other religions). Why this attempt? Because the Jews refused to accept

---

44. Ibid., pp. 38–39.
45. I note that Catholic readers will recognize the issue of dual loyalty all too well, having long been accused of the same charge.

Antiochus as a god, would not tolerate the desecration of the Holy Temple, and would not allow themselves to be forced to violate their dietary and other religious laws.

Christian Antisemitism: Theologically, understanding Christian antisemitism seems straightforward. Jesus was a Jew whose message was directed to other Jews. Those Jews who didn't become Christian rejected this teaching. As a result, Jews in the early days of Christianity, and in every age since, represent a challenge to the doctrine that the Hebrew Bible clearly and unambiguously points to Jesus as Messiah and God incarnate. We Jews read the same Hebrew scripture as do Christians, hold these same words to be holy, and yet come to very different conclusions regarding their meaning.

This situation is exacerbated by several especially troubling elements in the Christian scripture. Such elements are understandable when we consider that the Christian Bible was written during the period of maximum competition between Jews and Christians. For Christianity to be correct, Judaism (or at least the Pharisees) had to be discredited. (It's worth noting that this competition was not one-sided. In the central *Amidah* prayer, the rabbis of Talmudic times inserted a prayer cursing *minim,* or heretics. Many scholars believe that this prayer was created specifically as an anti-Christian polemic designed to keep the early Christians from attending the synagogue service.[46]) Thus Matthew seems to depict the Jews as taking the blame for the crucifixion of Jesus. And not only the Jews of that time, but the Jews of all time share the guilt. "Then answered all the people and said, His blood be on our heads and the heads of our children" (Matt 27:25). Perhaps the early Christians were also trying to minimize the role of Pontius Pilate and Rome in the execution of Jesus so as to court favor with their Roman governors during this critical period. [47] Nonetheless, this verse created the seed for the idea that the Jew, no matter when he lived, is a "Christ-killer." John planted a second recurring theme in this vein, that of Jews' identification with the forces of evil: "Ye are of your father the devil, and your will is to do your father's desires" (John 8:44).

These elements were seized upon and amplified by the early leaders of the church. Listen to the words of Saint John Chrysostom

46. A. E. Milgram, *Jewish Worship,* Jewish Publication Society, 1971, p. 105.
47. *Encyclopaedia Judaica,* op. cit., vol. 3, p. 99.

of Antioch, archbishop of Constantinople, a fourth-century church father:

> Their synagogue or school is to be set on fire....Second, their houses are to be torn down and destroyed in the same way....Third, they are to have all their prayerbooks and Talmudics taken from them....Fourth, they are to be forbidden henceforth to teach...and praise God, to thank (God), to pray (to God), to teach (of God) among us and ours....Fifth, the Jews are to be deprived totally of walkway and streets....Are they not "inveterate murderers, destroyers, men possessed by the devil."...God hates the Jews and always hated the Jews....It is the duty of Christians to hate the Jews.[48]

In his early writings, Martin Luther, the founder of Protestant Christianity, spoke favorably of the Jews, believing that the excesses of the Catholic Church were a barrier to mass Jewish conversion to Christianity. In "That Jesus Christ Was Born a Jew," written in 1523, he hopes that

> perhaps I will attract some of the Jews to the Christian faith. For our fools—the popes, bishops, sophists, and monks—the coarse blockheads! have until this time so treated the Jews that to be a good Christian one would have to become a Jew....I would advise and beg everybody to deal kindly with the Jews and to instruct them in the Scriptures; in such a case we could expect them to come over to us.[49]

Now read what Luther writes just twenty years later, reacting to the fact that Jews have remained Jewish. In "Concerning the Jews and their Lies," he writes:

> What then shall we Christians do with the damned, rejected race of Jews?...First, their synagogues or

---

48. H. J. Cargas, *Shadows of Auschwitz: A Christian Response*, Crossroad, 1992, pp. 11–12.

49. *Readings in the Jewish-Christian Encounter*, F. E. Talmage, Editor, KTAV Publishing, pp. 33–34.

churches should be set on fire....And this ought to be done for the honor of God and Christianity in order that God may see that we are Christians, and that we have not wittingly tolerated or approved of such public lying, cursing, and blaspheming of His Son and His Christians. Secondly, their homes should likewise be broken down and destroyed....Thirdly, they should be deprived of their prayer-books and Talmuds in which such idolatry, lies, cursing, and blasphemy are taught. Fourthly, their rabbis must be forbidden under threat of death to teach any more....Fifthly, passport and traveling privileges should be absolutely forbidden to the Jews....Sixthly...all their cash and valuables of silver and gold ought to be taken from them....If, however, we are afraid that they might harm us personally,...then let us apply the same cleverness (expulsion) as the other nations, such as France, Spain, Bohemia, etc....For, as has been said, God's rage is so great against them that they only become worse and worse through mild mercy, and not much better through severe mercy. Therefore away with them...and we may be free of this insufferable devilish burden—the Jews.[50]

Although the stated purpose of the Crusades of the eleventh and twelfth centuries was to capture and free the holy land from the Muslims, when the Crusaders encountered Jews during their travels, they sometimes offered the Jews the choice of conversion or death. Although local bishops tried to protect them, entire Jewish communities were massacred with only a few accepting baptism. The Crusades caused many Jews to flee to Eastern Europe (especially Russia and Poland), where future centuries of persecution would await.

Also prominent in the story of Christian antisemitism from the Middle Ages to the present time are three classic libels leveled against Jews, once believed by many Christians in spite of the popes' repeated condemnation of the charges:

1. *Ritual Murder:* The lie, spread first in the twelfth century, was that Jews required the blood of Christians, especially in connection with the Passover holiday. The idea was that Jews

---

50. Ibid., pp. 34–36.

were trying to re-create the murder of Jesus. This libel has resulted in both individual Jews and entire Jewish communities being put on trial and executed, in spite of the fact that Jewish law specifically prohibits the consumption of *any* blood from *any* animal. It is noteworthy that Pope Gregory X, in his "letter on Jews" (1272), rejected Jewish guilt in these cases, saying, "Most falsely do these Christians claim that the Jews have secretly and furtively carried away these children and killed them....We order that Jews seized under such a silly pretext be freed."[51]

2. *Plots to Poison Christians:* The culmination of this libel was the accusation that Jews were responsible for the Black Death, which killed one-third of Europe's population in 1348–49. The verdict of one Swiss court held all Jews over the age of seven responsible for the plague and subject to execution. Children under seven were baptized and raised as Christians.[52] Needless to say, the murder of anyone, Jew, Christian, or otherwise, is prohibited by Jewish law in the strongest possible terms. It is the only crime for which capital punishment is specified in every book of the Torah.

3. *Desecration of the Host:* In the thirteenth century, transubstantiation, the miraculous transformation of the communion wafer into the actual body of Jesus, became Catholic Church dogma. Soon thereafter, Jews were accused of stealing and torturing these wafers, leading to the torture and murder of thousands. To cite but a few examples: in 1243, all of Berlitz's Jews were burned alive for this crime. In Prague in 1389, three thousand Jews were murdered, while in Berlin in 1510, twenty-six Jews were burned and two beheaded. Of course, no Jew would have believed that such a wafer was anything other than a wafer.

Lest we think that the kinds of things described above can be consigned to the dustbins of history, reflect that most observers agree that while Nazism was not Christian (indeed it was *anti*-Christian), the Holocaust could not have taken place without the history of almost two millennia of antisemitism. Speaking about the historic document "We

---

51. Cited by J. Carroll, *Constantine's Sword,* Houghton Mifflin, 2001, p. 273.
52. Prager and Telushkin, *Why the Jews,* op. cit., p. 102.

Remember: A Reflection on the Shoah," Cardinal John O'Conner stated: "While recognizing that the roots of Nazi anti-semitism grew outside the Church, it [the document] also addresses unambiguously and directly the erroneous and unjust application of church teaching on the part of many, which led, at least in part, to a climate which made it easier for the Nazis to carry out their Holocaust."[53]

In response to the Holocaust, Christians everywhere are reexamining their role and the role of their churches. In 1994, the Evangelical Lutheran Church in America, representing more than five million Lutherans, adopted an important resolution that repudiated the writings of Martin Luther. It said in part:

> Lutherans…feel a special burden in this regard because of certain elements in the legacy of the reformer Martin Luther and the catastrophes, including the Holocaust of the twentieth century, suffered by Jews in places where Lutheran churches were strongly represented. We…must with pain acknowledge also Luther's anti-Judaic diatribes and violent recommendations of his later writings against the Jews….We reject this violent invective….We express our deep and abiding sorrow over its tragic effects on subsequent generations….We particularly deplore the appropriation of Luther's word by modern anti-Semites for the teaching of hatred toward Judaism or toward the Jewish people.[54]

In a statement of contrition, the French Catholic Church, through its spokesman Olivier De Barranger, acknowledged that "it is of utmost importance to recognize the role, indirect if not direct, played by the anti-Jewish teachings, guiltily perpetuated by the Christian people, in the historical process that led to the Holocaust. On this soil flowered the venomous plant of the hatred of the Jews."[55] Statements like these and others are a welcome change from immediate postwar reactions such as the following: "In 1948, the German Evangelical Conference at Darmstadt [Germany]…proclaimed that

53. Cardinal J. O'Conner, "A Step Forward in an Ongoing Dialogue," in *Catholics Remember the Holocaust,* United States Catholic Conference, 1998, p. 59.

54. A. James Rubin, *A Jewish Guide to Interreligious Relations,* The American Jewish Committee, 1996, pp. 44–45.

55. "The French Church Repents," *The Jerusalem Report,* March 19, 1998.

the terrible Jewish suffering in the Holocaust was a divine visitation and a call to the Jews to cease their rejection and ongoing crucifixion of Christ."[56]

Muslim Antisemitism: Muslim antisemitism has much in common with the Christian experience. Although Islam[57] did not depend on Judaism in the same way as Christianity did, it has much in common with Judaism. Islam's great prophet, Muhammad, believed that the revelations to the Jews (the Hebrew Bible) and the Christians (the Christian Bible), although from *Allah* (the Arabic word for God) Himself were nevertheless imperfect precursors of the Qur'an, the Muslim book of divine revelation. The Qur'an shares much with both Hebrew and Christian scriptures. Muslims trace their faith back to the same Abraham of Judaism and Christianity, making all three of these monotheistic faiths members of the same family. Like the early Christians and Martin Luther, Muhammad believed that once the Jews heard the story of the latest revelation, they would convert to the new religion. In fact, initially Muhammad mandated a fast for Muslims on *Yom Kippur* (the Jewish Day of Atonement) and instructed them to pray in the direction of Jerusalem (also Jewish practice).[58] It was only after Jews refused to convert that the Muslims became hostile to Judaism and changed their direction of prayer to Mecca and their fast period to the entire month of Ramadan (at which time they observe daytime fasts).

Why did the Jews at the time reject the new Muslim faith? An important reason is that the "corrections" to the Hebrew scriptures that the Qur'an incorporated were seen by Jews as errors. Prager and Telushkin sum up the Jewish perspective regarding Islam and Christianity: "what was true in their [Muhammad's and Jesus'] messages was not new, and that what was new was not true."[59] The resultant anger at the Jews (and Christians, for that matter) seems to have been incorporated into the Qur'an. An important example is to be found in sura (chapter) 2, verse 61: "They [the Jews] were covered with humiliation and misery; they drew on themselves the wrath of God. This because they went on rejecting the Signs of God and slaying

---

56. Quoted in Cargas, *Shadows of Auschwitz,* op. cit., p. 45.
57. *Islam* is the name of the religion to which *Muslims* adhere.
58. Armstrong, *A History of God,* op. cit., p. 153.
59. Prager and Telushkin, *Why the Jews,* op. cit., p. 113.

His Messengers without just cause. This because they rebelled and went on transgressing." However, it would be misleading to imply that the bulk of Qur'an is antisemitic; other passages reflect far more tolerance. Consider this verse (sura 2, verse 62): "The Believers, the Jews, the Christians, and other monotheists, all who believe in God and the Last Day and do good will be rewarded by their Lord; they need not fear anything nor be despondent."[60]

Nonetheless, Jews and Christians were still seen in a better light than adherents of other religions. As the forces of Islam conquered Arabia and other lands, Jews and Christians, as "peoples of the Book" (i.e., monotheistic recipients of divine revelation), were given special status. While infidels (nonmonotheists) were given the choice of conversion or death, Christians and Jews "enjoyed" the status of *dhimmis* (meaning "protected"). This meant that they could maintain their religions so long as they agreed to be subservient to Muslims in their dress, actions, payment of special taxes, and so on. In practice, this meant harsh treatment of Christians and Jews, though not so harsh as Christian treatment of Jews. Perhaps there was reduced animosity since the Qur'an did not depend on a specific reinterpretation of the Bible.[61] In any event, the result was that virtually all Christian communities under Muslim domination (with the important exception of the Copts) disappeared while Jewish communities flourished.[62] (Some suggest that Jews had learned to adapt to living under a hostile majority culture. For Christians, however, such a subservient status was incompatible with their view of the truth of Christianity.) Indeed, the Middle Ages in Muslim Spain has been called the "Golden Era" of Judaism because of the relative freedom and creativity Jews enjoyed during this period.

In more modern times, Muslim antisemitism has been focused on opposition to Jewish settlement in Palestine and the resultant creation of the State of Israel. Repeatedly, the Arab/Muslim nations surrounding Israel have attacked with the stated goal of destroying the State and driving the Jews into the sea. As a leading contemporary Arab scholar sums up, "the existence of the Jews was not a provocation to Islam...as long as Jews were subordinate or

---

60. K. Duran, *Children of Abraham: An Introduction to Islam for Jews,* KTAV Publishing House, 2001, p. 113.

61. *Encyclopaedia Judaica,* op. cit., vol. 3, p. 99.

62. Prager and Telushkin, *Why the Jews,* op. cit., p. 116.

degraded. But a Jewish state is incompatible with the view of Jews as humiliated or wretched. The call for a Palestinian Arab state in place of Israel is for a state in which once again 'Islam dominates and is not dominated.'" [63] In spite of the fact that during World War II most Arab leaders were pro-Nazi, the postwar Western world largely supported Arab claims to Palestine. Arab control of a large portion of the world's oil was no doubt responsible. In the mid-1990s, in the wake of peace treaties between Israel and Egypt and Israel and Jordan, the continuing peace process leading to the creation of a Palestinian state in the West Bank and Gaza, the establishment and growth of an indigenous, independent, and proud Israeli Arab Muslim movement whose adherents saw themselves as loyal citizens of the Jewish state, there was room for cautious optimism for future Muslim-Jewish relations. More recent events are less hopeful, however.

Enlightenment and Leftist Antisemitism: To this point, our focus on historical antisemitism has been theological, stemming from Judaism's religious competition with pagan, Christian, and Muslim religions. One might therefore conclude that the arrival of the Enlightenment and ascendancy to power of socialism and communism, all distinctly secular movements, would signal an end to antisemitism. Unfortunately, these movements just changed the focus of antisemitism—from the God component of Judaism to its national component. Listen to the words of no less a democratic icon than France's François Voltaire on the subject on Jews and Judaism: "(Jews are) the most abominable people in the world....They are a totally ignorant nation who, for many years, have combined contemptible miserliness and the most revolting superstition with a violent hatred of all those nations that have tolerated them."[64] Similar hostility was seen in Germany and England. Although no violence was to accompany the antisemitism of the Enlightenment, by the early twentieth century, the religious and antireligious movements of Europe could agree on one thing: that Judaism and the Jews should be driven from the planet.

Karl Marx, the father of socialism and communism, was the product of a long line of rabbis on both sides of his family. Baptized a

---

63. Ibid., p. 123.
64. Ibid., p. 128.

Lutheran as a child (his father had converted in order to be able to continue practicing law under newly enacted Prussian laws),[65] his writings on Judaism are no less kind than those of Martin Luther: "What is the secular cult of the Jew? *Haggling.* What is his secular god? *Money.* Well then! Emancipation from *haggling* and *money,* from practical, real Judaism would be the self-emancipation of our time....Money is the jealous God of Israel, beside which no other God may stand."[66] Not surprisingly, virtually all Marxist governments have been antisemitic. Soviet antisemitism is legendary; it was only after the demise of the Soviet Union that Russian Jews were allowed to practice their religion openly and emigrate to Israel.

Nazi Antisemitism: Nazi antisemitism was unique in that it did not offer the Jew the opportunity of conversion or assimilation. It is also unique in the depth and scope of its cruelty and success in murdering Jews. It is well beyond the scope of this book to present a thorough discussion of Nazi antisemitism and the Holocaust. Sources for a deeper study of these topics are presented in the bibliography. My goal is simply to dispel some common misconceptions about Nazi antisemitism and to give you a sense of the magnitude of the Holocaust.

1. *On the Myth That Nazi Antisemitism Was Simply Racism:* Although the Nazis were racist, racism was a tool they used to pursue their hatred of Jews rather than its cause. First and foremost, Jews are not a race. There are Jews of every race and one can become a Jew irrespective of one's race. Second, Arab Semites were not considered to be enemies of the Nazis and Nazis had no problem working with such non-Aryans as the Japanese and the Italians. In the case where the Nazis attacked the Gypsy "race," they murdered only the mixed Gypsy products of intermarriage and exempted the "racially pure" from extermination. More than 14,000 were deliberately spared.[67]

65. Ibid., p. 137.
66. Ibid., p. 138.
67. Y. Bauer, "The Place of the Holocaust in Contemporary History" in *Holocaust: Religious and Philosophical Implications,* J. Roth and M. Berenbaum, Editors, Paragon House, 1989, pp. 16–44.

2. *On the Myth That Antisemitism Was a Tool to Win Support for the War—It Made the Jews Scapegoats:* As incredible as it sounds, there is convincing evidence to support the idea that Hitler pursued the war in order to destroy the Jews rather than the reverse. Late in the war when railroad cars were in short supply to transport troops, not a single car was diverted from its death camp duty, nor a single troop diverted from its task of murdering Jews. "When a Nazi general, Kurt Freiherr von Grienanth, gingerly noted in September 1942 that 'the principle should be to eliminate the Jews as promptly as possible without impairing essential war work,' he was demoted by Heinrich Himmler, the chief of the Gestapo, who denounced the general's proposal as a subtle effort to support the Jews."[68] Shortly before his suicide, Hitler addressed the German people: "Above all I charge the leaders of the nation and those under them to scrupulous observance of the laws of race and to the merciless opposition to the universal poisoner of all peoples, international Jewry."[69]

3. *Impact on the Jewish People:* Most of us know that some six million Jews, including more than a million children, were murdered in the Holocaust—about a third of the Jews then alive. Less known is the fact that some 50 percent of Europe's Jews, including some 80 percent of the rabbis and full-time students of Judaism then alive, were murdered.[70] At the time of the Holocaust, the center of Jewish teaching and study was in Europe. The impact of the loss of this leadership is felt to this day.

4. *Jews Had No Place to Go:* The history of the period is replete with instances of nation after nation refusing to allow Jews to enter. One particularly bitter example concerns the voyage of the ship *St. Louis* to North America. In May 1939, 937 Jews had passage paid and had visas secured for entry into Cuba. A change in the Cuban government resulted in the cancellation of the visas, and the ship literally went up and down the coastline of the Americas with no country (not even the United

68. Prager and Telushkin, *Why the Jews,* op. cit., p. 156.

69. Cited in L. Dawidowicz, *War Against the Jews, 1933–1945,* Holt, Rinehart and Winston, 1975, p. 22.

70. I. Greenberg, *The Jewish Way,* Summit Books, 1988, pp. 315 and 326.

States) allowing them to enter. Finally several European countries (England, Belgium, Holland, and France) agreed to admit them. Those Jews fortunate enough to have been selected by England survived the war. After the war, however, Great Britain would not allow large numbers of survivors of the Holocaust to enter Palestine. One of the first and most important laws passed by the new State of Israel was the Law of Return, admitting for automatic entry and citizenship any and all Jews.

5. *Cooperation of the Local Populations:* The record is painful. Those nations that asserted that Jews were its citizens and refused to cooperate with the Nazis saved almost all their Jews. Denmark, Finland, and Bulgaria are examples. In contrast, countries such as Poland, with a deep history of antisemitism, saw 90 percent of its Jewish citizens murdered. Most of the Nazi death camps were located in Poland. And even after the war, the murder continued. In commemorating the fiftieth anniversary of the July 1946 murder of forty-two Jews returning to Kielce, Poland, Polish Prime Minister Wlodzimierz Cimoszewicz told the town's citizens that "we are obliged to accept the legacy of our history, deeply regretting everything that Poles have ever been guilty of against Jews."[71]

6. *Christian Response:* While individual priests and ministers did much to save Jews, many did little or nothing. Although Pope Pius XI declared that all Christians, as children of Abraham, are themselves "spiritual Semites," and, in 1937 issued an encyclical, *Mit Brennender Sorge* ("With Burning Sorrow"), condemning the racialism of Nazi ideology as opposed to Catholic doctrine,[72] the Holy See's Commission for Religious Relations with the Jews statement of March 1998 stated: "Did Christians give every possible assistance to those being persecuted and in particular to the persecuted Jews? Many did, but others did not."[73]

---

71. "Polish Leader Marks Anniversary of Jewish Massacre," *Los Angeles Times,* July 8, 1996, p. A8.

72. Archbishop O. Lipscomb, "Commemorating the Liberation of Auschwitz," in *Catholics Remember the Holocaust,* United States Catholics Conference, 1998, p. 17.

73. "We Remember: A Reflection on the *Shoah,*" in *Catholics Remember the Holocaust,* United States Catholics Conference, 1998, pp. 52–53.

7. *Magnitude of the Horror:* I have seen the films, I have read the books, I have visited four of the concentration camps, I have met numerous survivors. Many of you have probably seen the film, *Schindler's List.* As difficult as this film is to watch, a concentration camp survivor once told me that the film only shows one-hundreth of the horror, but he didn't object because no one would be able to bear to see even a few minutes of the true picture. I offer one small glimpse from the pages of testimony at the Nuremberg war crimes trial. On the stand was a Polish guard at Auschwitz who described one particular technique that was used to sustain the Auschwitz death machine in its "production" of some 10,000 murders per day:

> WITNESS: Women carrying children were [always] sent with them to the crematorium. [Children were of no labor value so they were killed. The mothers were sent along, too, because separation might lead to panic, hysteria—which might slow up the destruction process, and this could not be afforded. It was simpler to condemn the mothers too and keep things quiet and smooth.] The children were then torn from their parents outside the crematorium and sent to the gas chambers separately. [At that point, crowding more people into the gas chambers became the most urgent consideration. Separating meant that more children could be packed in separately, or they could be thrown in over the heads of adults once the chamber was packed.] When the extermination of the Jews in the gas chambers was at its height, orders were issued that the children were to be thrown straight into the crematorium furnaces, or into pits near the crematorium, without being gassed first.

> SMIRNOV [Russian prosecutor]: How am I to understand this? Did they throw them into the fire alive, or did they kill them first?

> WITNESS: They threw them in alive. Their screams could be heard at the camp. It is difficult to say how many children were destroyed in this way.

SMIRNOV: Why did they do this?

WITNESS: It's very difficult to say. We don't know whether they wanted to economize on gas, or if it was because there was not enough room in the gas chambers.[74]

8. *Could It Happen Again? Could It Happen Here?:* Based on my own experience, I don't believe the Holocaust could happen again, certainly not here in the United States. I feel very safe, as safe as loyal Jewish Germans felt at the time of the Hitler's rise to power. On the question, "Could it happen here?" we should reflect on the results of the Milgram experiment.[75] The study involved a psychology experiment set up so that an "assistant" to a doctor would administer electric shocks to the "subject" when a question was answered incorrectly. The actual subject, however, was the person who thought he was the assistant. The person who seemed to be receiving the shocks was an actor and no electrical shocks were actually delivered. The study found that most ordinary New Haven, Connecticut citizens (the study took place at Yale University) were willing to continue administering electric shocks to subjects, notwithstanding the subjects' cries, pleas, and, sometimes, even feigned unconsciousness. It appears that the presence of an authority figure assuring them that what they were doing was proper was sufficient to allow them to torture their fellow human being. Could it happen here?

We will probably never fully understand the Holocaust. It is so bizarre, so horrible, so incredible that many deny it ever happened. People who were young adults during this period are now in their eighties. If you have a chance to hear a speaker who was a witness to this time, make a special attempt to attend. Today's children are the last to be able to meet survivors of the Holocaust face to face and, for this reason, oral and videographic histories are being recorded in their own words.

---

74. Quoted in Cargas, *Shadows of Auschwitz,* op cit., p. 36.
75. S. Milgram, "Some Conditions of Obedience and Disobedience to Authority," *Human Relations* 18 (1965), pp. 57–75.

JEWISH MISTRUST OF CHRISTIANITY

I have told you this story of 2,500 years of horror in order to make you more sensitive to many Jews' response to Christianity, to help you understand that although Christians can love and embrace Judaism as the religion of Jesus, it is very hard for Jews to feel warmth for Christianity. I have spoken at literally scores of Christian churches and schools about Judaism and its beliefs. I have never seen a member of the Christian clergy or even a Christian layperson invited to a Jewish venue for a presentation about Jesus or Christianity. (I have seen Christians speak in synagogues about history, the Holocaust, brotherhood, a neutral biblical topic, or the aftereffect of an incident of antisemitism.) Jews, even those who have not been the target of Christian missionaries, even those who are not particularly observant, recoil when a Christian wants to "share the good news about Jesus." I know Jews whose sole Jewish passion is making sure that Hanukkah gets equal time with Christmas in any public school activities. Jews, notwithstanding the Jewish mission to teach the world about God and God's commandments, are often at the forefront of fighting the posting of those commandments in public places or allowing school prayer. Their fear of forced religious instruction and conversion is still very real.

Please understand. We carry the national memory of how Christianity and other religions have been used, not as a tool to find God, but as an instrument of torture. The legacy of the Holocaust for Christians and Christianity must include reexamination of how its teachings may have paved the way to the murder of six million innocents. I take great comfort in the words of Pope John Paul II, spoken at his historic visit to Jerusalem's Yad Vashem Holocaust Museum:

> As Bishop of Rome and Successor of the Apostle Peter, I assure the Jewish people that the Catholic Church, motivated by the Gospel law of truth and love and by no political considerations, is deeply saddened by the hatred, acts of persecution and displays of anti-Semitism directed against the Jews by Christians at any time and in any place....In this place of solemn remembrance, I fervently pray that our sorrow for the tragedy which the Jewish people suffered in the twentieth century will lead to a new relationship between Christians and Jews. Let us build a

new future in which there will be no more anti-Jewish feeling among Christians or anti-Christian feeling among Jews, but rather the mutual respect required of those who adore the one Creator and Lord, and look to Abraham as our common father in faith.[76]

Amen.

76. Speech of John Paul II, visit to Yad Vashem Museum, March 23, 2000, from the Vatican web site.

7
Jewish Practice in Lots of Nutshells

Judaism is a way of life, Jewish living a mosaic composed of hundreds and thousands of individual customs, holidays, and practices. In this chapter, I provide a description of the most significant of these in a "nutshell." Those items identified with an asterisk (*) are also discussed in the following chapter, which will help you prepare for actually going to these celebrations.

A word about the differences in the Jewish community that you are likely to encounter is in order. There are several kinds of differences:

- **The Movements:** The four major movements in Judaism—Orthodox, Reform, Conservative, and Reconstructionist—are described in the section "Worship and Prayer" below. As you will see, the approach of these various movements to Jewish ritual and law varies considerably.
- **Ashkenazi versus Sephardi:** The Jewish community is divided further by the place of origin of the Jews themselves. Jews coming from Eastern and Western Europe are Ashkenazic (Hebrew for the area we now call Germany) and Jews tracing their ancestry to Southern Europe, especially Spain or the Arab world and the Middle East, Sephardic (from the Hebrew word for Spain). The overwhelming majority of North American Jews are Ashkenazi in origin. As you will learn in this chapter, the two groups vary in terms of culture, their customs of observance, and their pronunciation of the Hebrew language.
- **Israel versus Diaspora:** Beyond these differences, there are some practices that Jews living in the land of Israel will observe differently from those living in other lands (called the diaspora). These are not stressed in the discussion below.

THE CYCLE OF LIFE

1. Circumcision and Baby-Naming*: As we have seen, Judaism is a religion of covenant, a mutual commitment and set of obligations that Jews as a people, and each of us individually, has with God. The Hebrew word for "covenant" is *Brit* (in Ashkenazic Hebrew and Yiddish, pronounced *Bris*) and the ceremony for recognizing a male baby as being in the *Brit* is called the *Brit Milah,* or "covenant of circumcision" (often, you will hear this shortened and referred to as a *Bris*). As specified in the Bible (Gen 17:9–14; 17:24–25; 21:4), Abraham was told by God to circumcise himself, his two sons, and "every male among you...as a sign of the covenant between Me and you." As God commanded Abraham, each baby's circumcision takes place at the age of eight days (some say so that at least one Sabbath will take place before the circumcision), with the actual removal of the foreskin traditionally performed by the *mohel,* an individual specially trained in both the medical and ritual requirements of the procedure. At the *Brit,* the baby boy receives his Hebrew name. Jews of Ashkenazi or Eastern European origin generally will name the baby after a deceased relative they wish to honor, whereas it is common for Sephardic Jews to name the child after a living relative.

Jewish baby girls often receive their Hebrew name at the synagogue a few weeks (traditionally within a month) after birth; one traditional custom is that the name is simply announced in connection with the father's being called to the Torah during services. Although Judaism does not mandate a specific ceremony similar to that of the *Brit Milah,* Reform Judaism, with its emphasis on equality between the sexes, has instituted a ceremony for welcoming baby girls into the covenant called *Brit Ha-Chayim* ("covenant of life") or *Brit Bat* ("covenant of the daughter"). Increasingly congregations in all the movements are experimenting with ceremonies to celebrate the entry of their daughters into the covenant.

2. Bar and Bat Mitzvah*: When a Jewish boy reaches the age of thirteen, and a Jewish girl reaches the age of twelve (thirteen in Reform practice), they are considered young adults, and, hence, according to our tradition, are obligated to observe Jewish law. Beginning in the Middle Ages, this rite of passage was observed by having the young man (there was no equivalent ritual for a young woman at the time) called up to offer blessings and, often, to read from the Torah scroll (see below for a discussion of the Torah and Torah scroll) during a regular morning service. Since this honor, called an *aliyah,* was reserved only for adult Jewish men, this act signified a boy's "coming of age" Jewishly. He was said to be a "son of commandment" (meaning someone responsible for its performance) or a *Bar Mitzvah.* In addition to reading from the Torah scroll, the *Bar/Bat Mitzvah* will also read a related passage from the one of the Biblical Prophets, called the *haftarah,* a practice observed on Sabbath mornings.

In modern times, this tradition includes young women (a young woman becomes a *Bat Mitzvah,* "daughter of commandment") and has become an occasion for a family celebration often involving parties and receptions. In our age where education is normally secular, the *Bar/Bat Mitzvah* signifies that a child has completed a course in Jewish learning and is now competent to conduct a prayer service as well as to read from the Torah. This requires a working knowledge of Hebrew and the structure of the prayer service. The *Bar/Bat Mitzvah* student will also normally provide a sermon on his or her learning experience as well as on the Torah portion of the week. (For more on Torah readings, see p. 83.)

3. Confirmation: Early in its history, Reform Judaism created a religious school graduation ceremony, or Confirmation, for older students in recognition that religious education should not stop at age thirteen. Confirmation ceremonies, common to virtually all Reform congregations and popular in some Conservative and Reconstructionist congregations as well, are group events honoring the entire graduating class of sixteen-year-old students. The ceremony takes place on or near the holiday of *Shavuot* (see below), since this holiday commemorates Moses' receiving the Torah on Mt. Sinai.

4. Marriage*: Marriage is considered by Judaism to be an event of particular holiness, so much so that one of the Hebrew names associated with the ceremony *(Kiddushin)* is derived from the Hebrew word for holy *(kadosh).* A man and a woman are traditionally considered to be separate, unfulfilled halves until they are joined in marriage. A modern Jewish wedding actually combines the religious ceremonies of betrothal, called *Kiddushin* or *Erusin,* and a second part, called *Nisuin* or marriage. The Talmud recognizes three ways that a wife is "acquired": by gift, by contract, and by cohabitation. All three are accomplished in the Jewish marriage ceremony: the gift is the presentation of the wedding ring (which, by tradition, should be solid so as to be unambiguous in its value), the contract is a written *ketubbah* or wedding contract, and cohabitation is symbolically accomplished by a brief period during which the bride (Hebrew *kallah*) and groom (Hebrew *chattan*) are left alone shortly after the formal ceremony.

The actual ceremony takes place under a *chuppah,* or wedding canopy, and may be in a synagogue, a home, or a catering hall, or even outdoors. The presiding rabbi welcomes and blesses the couple and ensures that the provisions of Jewish law are fulfilled. These include the signing and the reading of the *ketubbah,* giving of the ring or rings, pronouncement of the formula for acquiring a spouse, recitation of the prescribed seven blessings *(sheva berakhot),* and the traditional breaking of a glass by the groom at the end of the ceremony. This last "step," while not part of Jewish law, is an ancient custom. It may reflect superstitions about frightening away evil spirits or it may be a gesture to diminish our joy since the Temple in Jerusalem has not yet been rebuilt. Whatever the origin of the tradition, the breaking of the glass is the signal for the guests to shout *"mazel tov!"* ("congratulations/good luck") and for the postceremony celebrations to begin.

Judaism does provide for divorce in the event that the married couple proves to be incompatible. The divorce document is called a *get* and is written by the husband to the wife. The Reform movement does not require a specific Jewish divorce, recognizing civil divorce as binding, but does recognize the need to provide a religious closing with an optional "Document of Separation and Release."

5. *Death and Funerals*:* Judaism has many customs and laws dealing with death and funerals. When death claims our loved ones, when we are most upset and disoriented, it is comforting to be told exactly what to do and when to do it. Jewish tradition focuses on paying honor to the deceased from the moment of death (defined in Jewish law as the cessation of breathing) to the moment of burial, at which point the focus shifts to comforting the mourners. Tradition requires that the burial must take place as soon as possible, within a day if feasible, but never on the Sabbath or a holiday. Often the time is extended a day or two to allow family living in distant places to attend. Condolence calls to the family come only *after* the funeral, and viewings of the body do not normally take place.

The funeral is often conducted in a funeral home, with the ceremony taking place both in a funeral home chapel and at the graveside, but sometimes only at the cemetery. Eulogies are delivered by the rabbi and/or the deceased's family members and friends. Psalms and other prayers are recited and/or chanted in Hebrew and English in the chapel and at the graveside. Members of the immediate family (parents, siblings, spouse, and children) of the deceased wear a torn ribbon or actually tear their garments as a symbol of their mourning. At the graveside, the traditional Mourners' *Kaddish* prayer is said, and family members and attendees may ceremonially fill in the first bits of earth or even the entire grave. Cremation is strongly discouraged in Jewish tradition since the Bible tells us that we came from and will return to dust, and since traditional Judaism believes in physical resurrection (which is thought to be impaired by cremation). Furthermore, cremation is seen as disrespectful to the body of the dead and has a particularly negative connotation in the wake of the mass cremations of the Holocaust.

After the funeral, the family returns to the home where *shivah* (literally meaning "seven," referring to the seven days' duration of the most intense period of mourning) is observed. Upon their return from the cemetery, friends and relatives serve the immediate family the traditional meal of condolence, beginning a period of gradually integrating the reality of their loss into their lives. For the next seven days, the immediate family's mourners will traditionally sit on low seats and refrain from the normal activities of life, such as going to work, attending or viewing entertainment, and so on. Friends and families are expected to pay "*shivah* calls" to comfort the family. During this period, it is common for at least one of the three daily services to be held at the *shivah* home, with the required *minyan* (quorum of ten Jews) so that the Mourners' *Kaddish* may be recited. The overall effect is to ensure that the reality of death is faced by the family with the help, comfort, and support of extended family, friends, and the community. After the seven days of *shivah,* mourning continues to a lesser extent for the first thirty days (Hebrew *sheloshim*), during which mourners return to work but abstain from social engagements. Mourning continues for eleven months or a full year *(shana)* following the death of a parent, during which the Mourners' *Kaddish* is recited daily. Beyond this, families observe the anniversary (Yiddish *yahrzeit*) of the passing of their loved one by lighting special twenty four-hour *yahrzeit* candles, by reciting the Mourners' *Kaddish* prayer at worship services, and by giving to charity in the deceased's name. The above describes traditional mourning practices; you may find that less observant Jews will not observe them all.

HOLIDAYS AND THE JEWISH CALENDAR

The Jewish calendar is much more than a collection of months with Hebrew names sprinkled with varied holidays. It is the roadmap for Jewish spirituality and one of the keys to the preservation of the Jewish people. Rabbi Irving Greenberg has written an important book[77] that addresses the deeper spiritual meanings behind each of the holidays. In addition, any of the general introductions to Judaism listed in the bibliography provides a more detailed introduction to the holidays highlighted below.

1. Shabbat*: As the Hebrew author Ahad Ha-Am put it, "more than the Jews have kept the Sabbath, the Sabbath has kept the Jews." The Jewish Sabbath (Hebrew *Shabbat;* Ashkenazic Hebrew and Yiddish *Shabbos*) is one of the most sacred of the holy days of the calendar despite the fact that it comes once a week. On the Sabbath, we have an opportunity to reflect upon our lives, our accomplishments, our loves, our friendships, our families, and our inner spirit. This is in emulation of God, who rested from His labors after the six days of creation. "For in six days the LORD made heaven and earth and sea, and all that is in them, and He rested on the seventh day; therefore the LORD blessed the Sabbath day and hallowed it" (Exod 20:11). Like God, on the Sabbath we abstain from creating (that is, from active work); we do not try to change the world but try simply to be a part of the world. The Bible also teaches another reason for the Sabbath: "Remember that you were a slave in the land of Egypt and the LORD your God freed you from there with a mighty hand and an outstretched arm; therefore the LORD your God has commanded you to observe the Sabbath" (Deut 5:15). We abstain from working on the

---

77. I. Greenberg, *The Jewish Way,* op. cit.

Sabbath in order to reflect on creation, and because we remember what it meant to be slaves for whom work was endless.

The Torah specifies that we, our household, our servants, and even our animals will do no work on the Sabbath. The texts (Exod 20:9; Deut 5:13) command us to work for six days (a part of the fifth commandment that is often overlooked) and to abstain on the seventh day. Interestingly, the Bible does not tell us exactly what work is (beyond a very few forbidden activities like making a fire, leaving your settlement, planting and harvesting, and collecting *manna*). The more explicit definition of the categories of forbidden labor on the Sabbath is left to the Mishna (tractate *Shabbat* 2:2), where thirty-nine specific activities are defined as work. From these, the rabbis of the Talmud identified the wide range of activities an observant Jew must avoid on the Sabbath. To the non-Jew or nonobservant Jew, these restrictions seem onerous. Traditionally observant Jews will not drive, turn on an electrical appliance (even a light switch), turn on a gas oven or light any flame, carry objects (including keys, a child, a wallet) beyond a restricted geographical area, or use a telephone. To the observant Jew, the Sabbath is really about what he or she is now *free* to do having been exempted from all the routine drudgery of life. Without work to do, shopping to attend to, baseball and soccer games to carpool to, phone calls to return, and television to watch, one is free to enjoy a leisurely meal with family and friends, to study, worship, and rest without the time pressure of other things to do, to step back and reflect on the *products* of his or her labor rather than being continually caught up in the *process* of that labor.

We are taught that the Sabbath is a foretaste of the world to come, of the world redeemed. What would a perfect world be like? It would be a world where we wouldn't have to labor, where we wouldn't worry about money, where we could enjoy our friends and family, where we would take pleasure in good food, where we could pray and study at leisure; in short, it would be a continuous *Shabbat*. In the thousands of years that Jews have been struggling to bring about the age of redemption, we have had a once-a-week glimpse at the fruits of our labors: the Holy Sabbath. Rabbi Abraham Joshua Heschel's short book on the Sabbath[78] provides insight into the spirituality of the day. Another

---

78. A. J. Heschel, *The Sabbath: Its Meaning for Modern Man,* Farrar, Straus and Giroux, 1951.

book,[79] published by the Central Conference of American Rabbis (the rabbinic association of the Reform movement), is an excellent "how to" guide for those who want to begin deeper observance of the day.

The *Shabbat,* like any other holiday or, for that matter any day in the Hebrew calendar, begins at sundown (following the biblical description, "and there was evening and there was morning, day one"—Gen 1:5), in this case, on Friday night. In traditional homes, *Shabbat* candles (see figure 3) are lit by the woman of the house just before sundown, after which the family goes to a brief *Kabbalat Shabbat* ("welcoming the *Shabbat*") service at the synagogue. This is followed by a *Shabbat* dinner at home that is festive and elegant, often with the best china and silverware. Before the dinner, the *kiddush* blessing is said over the wine, praising and thanking God for providing the wine and the *Shabbat* itself (see figure 3). Blessings are shared among the family as husband and wife bless one another and both bless their children. This is followed by blessings over the specially braided *challah* bread and the meal itself. Following the meal and the grace after the meal are festive songs and discussion. Many synagogues will have their *Kabbalat Shabbat* ("receiving the Sabbath") services after dinner, followed by a social *Oneg Shabbat* ("delight of Sabbath") dessert of cakes, cookies, and other delicacies. On Saturday morning, there will be a full *Shabbat* service in which the Torah and *haftarah* are read. This is the most common time for *Bar* and *Bat Mitzvah* celebrations. In the afternoon, it is traditional to have a *Mincha* (afternoon) and *Ma'ariv* (evening) service combined, occasionally with a *Bar/Bat Mitzvah* celebration as well. The final Shabbat ceremony is *Havdalah* (Hebrew for separation), commonly performed in the home after sundown to signify the end of the *Shabbat.* If you have the good fortune to go to a Sabbath service, you will be greeted with *"Shabbat Shalom"* ("Sabbath peace to you") or the Yiddish *"gut Shabbos"* ("good Sabbath"). You should respond in kind.

2. *Rosh Hashanah (mid- to late September):* Unlike its secular counterpart, *Rosh Hashanah* (literally "the head of the year"), Jewish New Year's Day, is not a time for wild parties and raucous celebration. The day is the beginning of the *Yamim Nora'im* ("Days of Awe") that end with *Yom Kippur* (see below). *Rosh Hashanah* and *Yom Kippur* together are known as the "High Holy Days" and, similar to Christmas

---

79. M. D. Shapiro, *Gates of Shabbat,* CCAR Press, 1991.

Image copyright of SweetChild Software

Figure 3: *Shabbat* Candles, Wine for *Kiddush* and *Challah*

and Easter, are the two Jewish holy days on which synagogues overflow with those Jews who attend only these services during the year. The traditional greeting on this holiday is *"shana tova,"* meaning "a good year," which is a shortened form of *"le-shanah tova teek-a-tay-vu,"* which means "may you be inscribed for a good year." This refers to the metaphor of God keeping a Book of Life in which are inscribed the names of those who will prosper and those who will not in the coming year. Although the liturgy teaches that "on *Rosh Hashanah* it [meaning one's fate] is written and on *Yom Kippur* it is sealed," in the same prayer we learn that "repentance, prayer, and charity temper judgment's severe decree." Thus, the ten days between the two holidays are a time for reflecting, making amends, and giving to charity. Because Jews know of God's love and forgiveness, we are inspired to repent and forgive one another. As a sign of our confidence in God's graciousness, we traditionally eat apples and honey in hope and expectation of a good and sweet year.

The sounding of the *shofar* (ram's horn) is a unique element in the *Rosh Hashanah* service. The haunting sound is a wakeup call, a reminder of God's sovereignty, God's covenants with the Jewish people and humanity, and the *shofar* sounds heard once when the

Torah was given at Mt. Sinai (Exod 19:16) and that will be sounded in the messianic days. It also recalls the ram's horns caught in a thicket at the time of Abraham's willingness to sacrifice his son, Isaac (Gen 22:13). In fact, we read this section of the Torah on *Rosh Hashanah* to remind God of the merit of our father Abraham and to ask that some merit drawn from Abraham's faith be given to us. Another interesting ceremony enjoying renewed practice is *Tashlich* (Hebrew for cast away). In this ceremony on *Rosh Hashanah* afternoon, we gather to symbolically cast our sins into the ocean, or any other natural body of water, and to recite appropriate prayers.

3. Yom Kippur (late September to early October): The conclusion of the ten days of awe is *Yom Kippur,* the Day of Atonement. During the period from sunset to sunset, traditional Jews take on a complete fast (no food or water) and abstain from sex and bathing, wearing leather products, and use of cosmetics. Many Jews who are otherwise not very observant will fast during this period. Significantly, Jewish law specifies that anyone who is ill, frail, or pregnant should not fast and must eat during this period. Many Jews will spend the entire day in the synagogue to pray a greatly expanded liturgy of prayers that include confession of sin, promises of repentance, and pleas for forgiveness. The liturgy makes it clear that the *Yom Kippur* ritual only offers forgiveness for sins against God; for sins against one's fellow man, forgiveness is possible from God *only if* forgiveness has been received from the person sinned against.

The evening service opens with a hauntingly beautiful prayer called *Kol Nidre* ("All Vows"). While the prayer itself is obscure (many believe it refers to a time in which Jews were forced during the Spanish Inquisition to convert and would therefore pray to be released from these forced vows of loyalty to another religion), its melody and tradition make it a cornerstone of the evening service (which is often called the *Kol Nidre* service). During the afternoon of *Yom Kippur,* we remember our departed loved ones in a *Yizkor* ("remembrance") service. The very end of the *Yom Kippur* service and fast is marked by a final long blast of the *shofar.* We leave the synagogue to return to our homes for a joyous "break-the-fast" meal, confident that our prayers have been heard and our sins forgiven such that *at-one-ment* with God and other human beings has been achieved.

4. Sukkot and Simchat Torah (five days after Yom Kippur):
Sukkot derives its name from the hut or booth (Hebrew *sukkah,* plural
sukkot) that the family builds specifically for observance of this holiday
as prescribed in the Torah (Lev 23:42–43). The holiday commemorates
the wandering in the desert during biblical times and the flimsy struc-
tures that we dwelt in at the time. To re-create the experience, Jews
build a *sukkah* and eat their meals in it; some will even sleep in it. Many
American Jews do not build *sukkot* but fulfill the *mitzvah* of entering
the structure at a *sukkah* at their synagogues or at the home of a friend.
Since *Sukkot* also has an agricultural (harvest) origin, the *sukkah* may
be decorated with harvest fruits. Another distinctive custom of the holiday is the waving of the *lulav* (palm branch), willow, myrtle, and *etrog*
(a citron, which looks like an elongated lemon) in fulfillment of the
commandment to rejoice before the Lord with these specific species
(Lev 23:40). The holiday of *Sukkot* lasts for seven days in Israel and
Reform practice, and for eight days in traditional diaspora communities. On the day following *Sukkot* (or on the last day of the holiday when
eight full days have been observed), we celebrate *Simchat Torah*
("rejoicing of the Torah") when, with great festivity (including dancing
with the Torah scrolls), we mark the renewal of the cycle of reading the
Torah. In a single breath, we conclude the book of Deuteronomy and
begin the book of Genesis to start the yearly reading cycle.

5. Hanukkah* (December): Although *Hanukkah* (often spelled
Chanukah) may be the most widely recognized Jewish holiday, it is
actually the only one in our list that is not mentioned in the Hebrew
Bible. The holiday commemorates the successful revolt of the Jews, led
by the Maccabee family, against the Hellenistic Syrian Empire in 165
B.C.E. The reigning emperor, Antiochus Epiphanes, forbade the observance of Judaism and desecrated the Holy Temple by sacrificing swine
and placing idols in it. The Hebrew word *Hanukkah* means "dedication" and celebrates the cleansing and rededication of the Temple once
the revolt was finally successful. Rabbinic tradition includes a legend
whereby there was only enough purified holy oil for the *ner tamid* (eternal light) for a single day. The miracle of *Hanukkah* was that the oil
lasted for eight days until additional oil could be prepared.

Today, *Hanukkah* is celebrated for eight days by lighting candles in
increasing numbers (that is, a "serving" candle plus one candle on the
first day, two candles on the second day, etc.) in a candelabra (Hebrew

menorah or *chanukiah;* see figure 9, p. 115). Children play a spinning top game called *dreidel* (in Yiddish, or *sivivon* in Hebrew) in which the four-sided top (called a *dreidel/sivivon;* see figure 10, p. 116) is spun to see which Hebrew letter will face up. The four letters, *nun, gimmel, hay, shin,* stand for the words *nes gadol haya sham,* meaning "a great miracle happened there."[80] Traditional foods eaten on *Hanukkah* are those made with oil (to heighten our consciousness of the miracle involving oil), including doughnuts and potato pancakes (called potato *latkes* in Yiddish). A traditional gift you will see is *Hanukkah Gelt,* or coins—either actual money or chocolate coins in foil wrappers. In countries such as the United States with a large Christian presence, the often close proximity of *Hanukkah* to Christmas has given the Jewish holiday an added popular significance and a tradition of gift giving. In areas with a significant Jewish population, stores, businesses, and schools are often careful to include *Hanukkah* celebrations and decorations along with those for Christmas. It's interesting to reflect that without *Hanukkah,* we might not have Christmas. That is, without the successful revolt in 165 B.C.E., Judaism might well have died out before the age of Jesus. If this were true, Jesus would not have been born a Jew and could not have been thought to be the Jewish Messiah. Most important, you should understand that Hanukkah is *not* the Jewish Christmas; it is a separate holiday with a distinct origin and observance.

6. Purim (late February to March): *Purim* is one of the happiest days of the Jewish calendar. It commemorates the survival of the fifth-century (B.C.E.) Jewish community in Shushan in Persia. As detailed in the biblical book of Esther, the wicked prime minister Haman's plot to kill all the Jews on a date selected by drawing lots (the Hebrew word for "lots" is *purim*) was foiled by Queen Esther and her cousin Mordecai. The entire scroll (Hebrew *megillah*) of Esther is read on *Purim* (this is the origin of the expression that you might have heard, "the whole *megillah*"); the reading is accented by noisemakers (called "groggers," or *ra-ah-shanim* in Hebrew) who shout every time the name of Haman is read, in an attempt to drown it out. Often, the rabbi, cantor, and other synagogue members will show up dressed in ridiculous costumes. Children will come dressed up as Queen Esther, Mordecai, or others in the story. It is a day when tradition commands

---

80. In Israel the Hebrew letter *shin* is replaced by a *pay* since the phrase must be changed to read that a "great miracle happened here" (the Hebrew word for "here" is *po*).

that we be joyous and unrestrained in our celebrations, as well as generous in our charity to the poor. We are also commanded to be friendly in our relations with our neighbors by sending portions of food to them. In North America, it is common for synagogues to hold *Purim* carnivals and parties for children. The traditional food of the holiday is a three-cornered pastry called *hamantashen* (literally "Haman's ears") filled with apricot, prunes, poppy seeds, or other fillings. *Purim* is also marked by *purimshpiels,* plays that poke fun at the *Purim* story, rabbis, and Jewish institutions in general.

7. Passover* (March to April): Passover (Hebrew *Pesach*) is, perhaps, the most widely celebrated of the Jewish holidays, with an estimated 90 percent of American Jews and 95 percent of Israeli Jews attending the traditional meal and associated rituals called the Passover *Seder.*[81] When I was growing up, we observed virtually no other Jewish holidays but we always had a traditional Passover *Seder.* Passover commemorates the exodus from slavery in Egypt and the act of God's angel of death "passing over" (the Hebrew word for "pass over" is *pesach*) the houses of the Children of Israel to spare them from the tenth plague, namely, the death of the first-born. It was following this plague that Pharaoh allowed the Hebrews to leave the land.

In their haste to leave, the Children of Israel did not have sufficient time to allow bread to rise; as a result, they had only unleavened bread called *matzah* (see figure 4). Thus, tradition commands that we eat *matzah* and no leavened products (called *chametz*) during Passover. In addition to leavened bread, *chametz* is defined as anything containing wheat, oats, rye, barley, and spelt that has not been certified as having kept its flour dry before cooking to prevent natural leavening. (Ashkenazi Jews also add legumes, corn, and rice to the list of forbidden foods.) In fact, the restriction against *chametz* is so strong that, during Passover, a Jew is not even allowed to own *chametz*. Small amounts are ceremoniously searched out and disposed of on the day before Passover, while larger amounts are sold to non-Jews for the duration of the eight-day holiday. Traditional Jews maintain a separate set of dinnerware, flatware, and pots and pans for Passover.

---

81. Wylen, *Settings of Silver,* op. cit., p. 136.

Image copyright of SweetChild Software

Figure 4: *Matzah*

The traditional Passover meal is called the *Seder,* a Hebrew word meaning "order," referring to the specified order of events, blessings, rituals, and readings that take place over the course of the evening. It is an excellent example of the home-based nature of Judaism. At the *Seder,* we read from a *Haggadah* (Hebrew for "the telling") as a script but often go off on tangents that bring home the message of freedom. The key elements of the *Seder* (and what to expect when you attend one) are described in the following chapter; the overall effect, however, is twofold. First, we fulfill a commandment that appears four times in the Torah: to "tell your children on that day" the story of the exodus from Egypt. Second, by repeating the story and eating the foods, we literally get a taste of slavery and redemption. We are commanded to feel that we were actually slaves in Egypt and were personally redeemed by God.

If you have an opportunity to attend a *Seder,* do so. You will be exposed to a wide range of beautiful Jewish traditions and interesting foods (see chapter 8 for details). Christians have a special interest in the Passover *Seder* since it is commonly believed that Jesus' Last Supper was a *Seder.* You may find that an interfaith *Seder* is being conducted in your community; check with your church.

8. Shavuot (May to June): The holiday of *Shavuot* (Hebrew for weeks) begins fifty days (or a week of weeks plus a day) after Passover. Although it, like all the Jewish festival holidays, has agricultural significance, its principal importance is to commemorate the giving of the Torah to Moses on Mt. Sinai. Traditional Jews formally count each day from the second day of Passover to *Shavuot* (this is called "counting the *omer*"; the *omer* was a measure of grain offered as a sacrifice in the Temple), firmly establishing the connection between freedom as celebrated on Passover and the receipt of the commandments from God as celebrated on *Shavuot*. A mystical tradition enjoying a revival in recent years is the *Tikun Leil Shavuot,* an all-night study session conducted on the night of the holiday. This holiday has also been chosen by many Reform and Conservative congregations for their Confirmation or graduation ceremonies.

9. The Jewish Calendar: Careful observers of Jewish holidays will notice that they do not fall on the same days of the standard (Gregorian) calendar each year. This is because the Jewish calendar is comprised of twelve lunar months. If it were not for the Torah telling us that Passover must occur in spring, the holidays, with their fixed dates in the Jewish calendar, would wander around and appear in any season. To keep Passover in the spring, the Jewish calendar has a nineteen-year cycle with an entire extra month added in seven of the nineteen years; this gives such years thirteen months instead of the normal twelve. In practice, this means that any Jewish holiday may come as much as three weeks earlier or later from year to year in the Gregorian calendar.

WORSHIP AND PRAYER

1. Movements: There are four movements within Judaism that you are likely to encounter in North America today: Orthodox, Reform, Conservative, and Reconstructionist. Most synagogues are affiliated with one of these movements. While the movements have different philosophies, members of these movements consider themselves to belong to the one Jewish people. Setting aside the issue of conversion and patrilineal descent (see discussion of "Conversion and Who Is a

Jew," below), a born Jew would be recognized as a Jew by members of any of the movements. The following is an extremely brief overview of the most significant differences among the movements:

a. Orthodox: Orthodox Jews would describe themselves as traditional or Torah Jews, holding that they are bound to Jewish law (Hebrew *halacha*) as divinely revealed in the Torah and Talmud, and as fixed by the medieval codes and interpreted by contemporary rabbinic authorities. An observant Orthodox man would, among other practices, keep his head covered (with a *kippah/yarmulke;* see figure 2, p. 28) and pray three times a day. Men and women would keep strictly kosher and not ride in an automobile on *Shabbat*. In Orthodox synagogues, men and women are seated in separate areas and only men are eligible to be active participants or to become rabbis and cantors. Services are conducted almost exclusively in Hebrew. These Jews believe that God's laws for us are applicable for all time; as the times change, we must find new ways to obey them and interpret them, but the fundamental laws do not change. Included within Orthodox Judaism is a wide range of groups, including Hasidic Jews. Hasidic Judaism was founded in the eighteenth century in Eastern Europe and is characterized by distinctive dress (see below) and appearance (for example, growing long side locks in accordance with Lev 19:27, which says "you shall not round off the side-growth on your head, or destroy the side-growth of your beard"), use of the Yiddish language, focus on joyous celebration of the relationship with God and on the special nature of each group's leader, their *rebbe*. The best known of these groups in the United States is *Chabad/Lubavitch*.

b. Reform: The Reform movement began as a reaction to the Enlightenment in Central and Western Europe early in the nineteenth century. It sought to find a path whereby Jews could better be a part of modern life and, concomitantly, maintain a distinctly Jewish identity. Today, many Reform Jews do not consider Jewish law (especially ritual laws) to be binding on their lives and, as such, generally do not observe *kashruth* (Jewish dietary laws), do not pray three times a day, and so on (although other Reform Jews are increasing their level of observance). Reform Jews place emphasis on the ethical teachings of the Prophets and stress the social action element of Judaism. They believe in complete equality of the sexes, have mixed seating at services, and ordain women as rabbis and cantors. There is wide variation in the nature of services, with a fluid mix of Hebrew and English. In general, Reform

Judaism places great responsibility on individual Jews to make decisions about their Jewish practice. Jewish law may be said to "have a vote but not a veto" in the Reform approach to religious practice.

c. Conservative: The Conservative movement grew to prominence early in the twentieth century with the waves of immigrants arriving in the North America from Eastern Europe. These Jews wanted to maintain the traditional Hebrew worship structure and the role of Jewish law, but wanted some accommodation to help in living their new lives in this modern land. Conservative Judaism tries to make changes in Jewish law only in a manner consistent with its historic development. For example, the Conservative rabbinate issued a *halachic* (Jewish legal) ruling allowing their members to drive on *Shabbat,* but only to and from synagogue. The movement is egalitarian and trains and ordains women as rabbis and cantors, and men and women sit together in synagogue.

d. Reconstructionist: This movement, founded by Mordecai Kaplan (1881–1984), does not believe in the traditional, supernatural God as a distinct personality and Creator, but holds that God is "the power that leads to salvation" and improvement in the world. It views Judaism as a civilization that nurtures and strengthens this impulse within us. It is therefore a movement that downplays the supernatural elements of God and stresses Jewish peoplehood and folkways. As in the case of Reform Judaism, it is a generally liberal movement and was, in fact, the first to endorse the idea of patrilineal descent (see "Conversion and Who Is a Jew," below).

2. The Synagogue: Not only do synagogues come in many sizes, shapes, and architectural styles, they come by many names. Reform congregations are likely to use the term *temple,* Conservative congregations, *synagogue,* and Orthodox, *shul.* They all share in common the fact that the synagogue (a Greek word translating the Hebrew phrase *beit knesset,* "house of assembly") is a center of prayer where men and women gather to pray and also to congregate and study. In every synagogue you will find the holy ark *(aron kodesh),* which contains the Torah scrolls, an eternal light *(ner tamid)* above the ark, and a raised area *(bimah)* for reading the Torah and conducting the services. You will probably also notice a memorial board, listing the names of congregants or relatives of congregants who have died and who are remembered especially on the anniversary of their death (there may be a small light next to the names that is lit on the anniversary of their passing). Usually, the building is oriented so that the congregation faces Jerusalem (east in North America) to pray. In Orthodox synagogues, there will be separate areas for men and women to sit. It is not unusual for synagogues to have schoolrooms, libraries, offices, and catering facilities adjacent to meet their congregation's needs.

If you are invited to visit a synagogue, dress as you would to visit any house of worship. At Orthodox and Conservative synagogues, you should expect to cover your head, men with a hat or *kippah* (see below) and women with a bit of lace; these will be provided for you if you do not bring your own. Chapter 8 provides more information regarding what to expect when you visit a synagogue.

3. Jewish Services, Liturgy, and the Siddur: The Jewish prayer-book, the *Siddur* (meaning "order"), is a collection of prayers that have been written over the past three thousand years. Some come directly from the Bible while others are as recent as those relating to the formation of the modern State of Israel in 1948 or even later. Most prayer-books that you will see in North America will include English translations of prayers, as well as prayers written in English that are not literal translations of the Hebrew. The *Siddur* will commonly include prayers for the various services on the Sabbath, on weekdays, and on holidays. Because of the extensive number of additional prayers on the High Holy Days, a special prayerbook called a *Machzor* is used for these services.

Traditional Jews pray three services each day: the morning or *Shacharit* service, the afternoon or *Mincha* service, and the evening or *Ma'ariv* service. In practice, a late afternoon service can be a double service, beginning as *Mincha* and ending as *Ma'ariv*. Traditional Jews require a quorum (called a *minyan*) of ten Jewish men (Reform and many Conservative include women in the *minyan*) to say certain prayers. On Saturdays, Mondays, and Thursdays, the Torah portion of the week is read or chanted from the Torah scroll. The service you are most likely to attend will be either an evening or morning Sabbath service.

There is a fixed order to the Jewish liturgy, and the basic structure of this liturgy is followed by all of the movements. After some introductory prayers, the congregation is formally called to worship with the words *"Bar'chu et Adonai Ha-Mevorach"* ("Bless God Who is

Blessed"), to which they respond *"Baruch Adonai Ha-Mevorach le-olam va-ed"* ("May God be blessed for ever and ever"). This is followed by prayers that introduce and articulate the central Jewish declaration of faith, *"Shema Yisrael, Adonai Eloheinu, Adonai Echad"* ("Hear, O Israel, the Lord is our God, the Lord alone"). Three prayers following this are the *Amidah* (the standing prayer), the *Aleinu* (a prayer looking forward to a time when all will recognize God as Lord), and the Mourners' *Kaddish* (a prayer for those in their first year's mourning cycle or those observing the anniversary of a loss of a loved one).

4. Torah: The Hebrew word *Torah* means "teaching" or "instruction." When Jews speak of the Torah in a narrow sense, we are referring to the first section of our Bible, specifically the first five books (Genesis, Exodus, Leviticus, Numbers, and Deuteronomy), also called the Five Books of Moses. The word *Torah* also refers to the sacred scroll that is the centerpiece of our worship service. In the broadest sense, Torah refers to all of Jewish sacred literature.

When you attend a Jewish worship service, you will notice the special reverence paid to the scrolls in the ark. The congregation rises when the ark is opened and, during certain prayers, bows in the direction of the ark. On the Sabbath (Friday night in many Reform congregations, Saturday morning in all congregations), one of the scrolls is taken from the ark and paraded around the sanctuary. Most worshipers will touch the Torah mantle (or covering) with their hand, their *tallit,* or their prayerbook, and then kiss the latter as a sign of reverence. There is no legal prohibition of non-Jews paying their respects in this way. The procession (called the *hakafah*) is said to be symbolic of the moment in which Moses brought the Torah to the Jewish people (tradition holds that the entire Torah was given to Moses on Mt. Sinai). The scroll is handwritten on the skin of a kosher animal by a special Jewish scribe called a *sofer* who requires as long as a year to complete a single scroll. A high point of the Sabbath service is when the leader calls various people to say blessings and/or read from the Torah scroll. At a *Bar* or *Bat Mitzvah,* the last reader will always be the child himself or herself.

Each week, the same section or *parasha* of the Torah is read in every synagogue of the Jewish world. A complete discussion of the Torah is well beyond the scope of this book. Alfred Kolatch has written a helpful book[82] discussing the Torah in a question-and-answer format.

---

82. A. J. Kolatch, *This Is the Torah,* Jonathan David Publishers, 1988.

Figure 5: *Tefillin* **and a** *Tallit*

5. *Garments:* At a Jewish worship service, you may notice that the men's heads are covered (this is optional in Reform services). The small circular hat, called a *kippah* in Hebrew but also commonly known by its Yiddish name, *yarmulke* (see figure 2), is worn as a sign of respect for God, and traditional Jewish men wear them at all times. The tradition of wearing one is a relatively recent, probably no more than a thousand-year-old custom. It is appropriate for non-Jewish men to wear the *kippah* at Jewish events where they are provided. If you go to a morning service, you will see (certainly Orthodox or Conservative, sometimes Reform and Reconstructionist) men and, often, women wearing a beautiful prayer shawl called a *tallit* or *tallis* in Ashkenazic Hebrew and in Yiddish (see figure 5). The commandment concerning this garment actually refers to the fringes at the corners of the garment, called the *tzitzit*. The Torah (Num 15:38–39) instructs us to wear these fringes on our cornered garments so that when we see them we will "recall all the commandments of the LORD and observe them." It's a bit like the old technique of tying a string around your finger to remember an especially important task. Orthodox Jews wear the *tzitzit* all day long; they are worn during the day only because the commandment refers to "seeing" them. It is almost certainly true that Jesus wore and prayed in *tzitzit;* Luke 8:44 appears to be a specific reference to the fringes. It is *not* appropriate for non-Jewish men or women to wear a *tallit,* since wearing this garment is a fulfillment of a specific Jewish law not considered binding on non-Jews.

You may also see another type of "garment" worn by traditional Jewish men during their weekday (i.e., non-Sabbath) morning prayers. These are the *tefillin* (the term is usually translated as "phylacteries") and they come in pairs, one for the head and one for the arm (see figure 5). They are worn to comply with the commandment (Deut 6:8) that we keep certain instructions bound "as a sign on your hand" and as "frontlets between your eyes." The *tefillin* consist of small black boxes containing four handwritten sections from the Torah (those verses where wearing *tefillin* are commanded); leather straps are used to bind the boxes to the hand and forehead. The *tefillin* are not worn on the Sabbath or on holidays.

Finally, you may see certain Orthodox Jews belonging to *Chabad* or to one of the other Hasidic sects of Judaism wearing unusual dress, including fancy fur hats and long black coats. Such dress, while not commanded by Jewish law, has become a custom for these groups and often reflects the traditional dress worn in the group's town of origin in Eastern Europe a hundred or more years ago.

6. Clergy: At most synagogues, you will find two Jewish clergy positions, the rabbi and the cantor. While these will always be men in Orthodox congregations, they may be men or women in any of the other movements. It is not uncommon for smaller congregations to lack one or both of these clergy persons. In this case, lay persons can fill in the role, with visiting clergy being used on High Holy Days, weddings, or other special occasions. As marriage and family are so central to Judaism, you will not be surprised to learn that rabbis and cantors are allowed and indeed encouraged to marry, establish homes, and raise families.

a. Rabbi: With the destruction of the Temple in 70 C.E., there was no longer a role for the *cohanim,* or priests, in Jewish worship. As prayer replaced sacrifice, the teacher or rabbi replaced the priest as principal Jewish authority. The role of the rabbi in both ancient days and today is as a teacher, officiant, and judge of Jewish law and tradition, serving the community. A rabbi is not specifically required by Jewish law for any Jewish service or life cycle event, but one often presides to ensure that the customs and requirements of tradition are met and, in the case of marriage ceremonies, to represent the government. Today, rabbis will have graduated from seminaries requiring four or five years of graduate-level studies. While many rabbis will go on to be engaged by congregations, others will work with students on college campuses or focus on teaching, hospital or prison chaplaincies, organizational work, or other roles in Jewish life. In a typical congregation, the rabbi (or rabbis—it is not uncommon to see two or more rabbis in larger congregations) is engaged by the board of trustees and usually works under a contract. Rabbinic duties usually extend beyond the congregation to service of the larger Jewish community and, of course, as a representative to the non-Jewish community. In addition to responsibilities in conducting services, the rabbi will also be heavily involved in counseling, in visiting the sick, and in teaching both children and adults about Jewish tradition.

b. Cantor: While the rabbi is the authority on Jewish law and texts, the cantor (Hebrew *chazzan*) is the specialist when it comes to the music and chanting of the liturgy. When you attend a Jewish service, you will notice that much of the liturgy is chanted with beautiful melodies. You probably do not know that many of the melodies are uniquely associated with not only the specific prayers but with the day of week (Sabbath versus holiday versus weekday) and time of day (morning, afternoon, or evening service). The cantor has been trained in these nuances and will lead the congregation appropriately. At many synagogues, the cantor will also be intimately involved in training the *Bar/Bat Mitzvah* student in the prayers and texts that will be read at his or her service.

JEWISH HOME AND JEWISH LIVING

With the destruction of the Holy Temple in 70 C.E., the home became a second focus for the practice of Judaism. While Jews meet, study, and pray in a synagogue, in a very real sense the heart of Jewish living is in our daily activities at home. When you visit a Jewish home, whether Reform, Conservative, Orthodox, or Reconstructionist, you will find a *mezuzah* on the entrance doorpost, *Shabbat* candlesticks, a *Hanukkah* menorah, a *tzedakah* box for charity, objects of Jewish art, and most of all, books. In the following "nutshells," we'll see how Judaism works in the day-to-day activities of Jewish life and in Jewish homes.

1. Mitzvot: 613 Commandments: The Hebrew word for "commandment" is *mitzvah* (plural *mitzvot*). Often, Jews and non-Jews will use the word to mean a good deed, but *mitzvot* are neither optional nor confined to ethical works. Under Jewish law, they define the action (or inaction) required in any of a wide variety of situations. Thus, a Jew visits the sick or pays a call on one who is in mourning not because his heart moves him (though indeed it may) but because he is commanded (by the Commander) to do so. We believe that God has given us the *mitzvot* as a sign of God's love for us so that we may best know how to live. As I noted earlier, the *mitzvot* enrich life and make a holy life possible in the same way that the net and court lines make a tennis game possible. No one suggests that tennis would be a more interesting, freer game if only we didn't have all the rules and that troublesome net. In the same way, the Jew doesn't long to be free of the *mitzvot*. Instead, we feel embraced and loved by God through them.

Jewish tradition recognizes 613 commandments enumerated in the Torah. Of these, less than three hundred are binding on us today since many refer to the sacrificial system no longer in practice while others are binding only in the land of Israel. For many *mitzvot* (though not all), one recites a blessing (Hebrew *bracha*) before performing the act.

2. Halacha: Although *halacha* is the Hebrew word meaning "Jewish law," a literal translation of the word is "the path." The term refers to the entire body of law and not just a single book or source. For traditional Jews, however, the single most important and authoritative source of *halacha* is the *Shulkhan Arukh,* compiled by Joseph Karo in the sixteenth century. With this and other codes as the core, Jewish law is periodically brought up to date with the resolution of specific questions of law by rabbinic authorities in what is called "*responsa* literature." In this way, we can resolve issues such as how to adapt traditional Jewish teachings to the modern realities of electricity, automobiles, airplanes, the Internet, and so on.

3. Kosher Foods: The word *kosher,* which is generally used to describe food that is acceptable for Jews to eat, has entered the English language to describe something that is okay or in order. A shaky business offering might prompt one to say, "This doesn't seem quite kosher to me." Ironically, this is quite consistent with the literal Hebrew meaning of the word, which is "fit." The basis for kosher foods is the Bible (Lev 11:3–23; Deut 14:4–21), with Talmudic teachings expanding the prohibitions to "make a fence around the Torah" (i.e., to ensure that inadvertent transgressions don't occur) as follows:

- **Meat:** The Bible tells us that we may eat any animal with cleft or split hoofs and that chews its cud. This means beef, veal, and lamb are kosher, and most other available meats (pork, rabbit, snake, etc.) are not. Talmudic law also specifies that only a qualified slaughterer, called a *shochet,* may slaughter meat or fowl in a specified way designed to minimize pain to the animal. This rule virtually eliminates hunting as a Jewish activity since no such food could be eaten, and hunting for pure sport would be an example of cruelty to animals. In addition, no blood may be eaten, and thus the meat must be prepared in a way to eliminate any remaining blood.
- **Poultry:** The Bible lists a number of birds that may not be eaten; all others are permitted. In practice, the meat of chicken, ducks, geese, turkeys, and pigeons are regarded as kosher if slaughtered in the proper manner.
- **Fish:** Only sea creatures with both fins and scales may be eaten. This prohibits shrimp, shellfish, lobster, eels, shark, catfish, and so on. Fish need not be ritually slaughtered.
- **Milk and Meat:** Three times (Exod 23:19; 34:26; Deut 14:21) the Bible states that "you shall not boil a kid in its mother's milk." The rabbis of the Talmud interpreted these verses to prohibit eating any milk product with any meat product and, in fact, to require that separate sets of dishes be used for meat (Hebrew *besari;* Yiddish *fleischig*) or dairy (Hebrew *halavi;* Yiddish *milchig*) foods. Foods that are neither meat nor dairy (fish, fruits, vegetables, etc.) are called *pareve* and may be eaten with either type of meal. Traditional Jewish homes will therefore have at least two sets of dishes (many will have four sets since we may not mix dishes for Passover with ordinary dishes), separate sinks, and even separate refrigerators.

Why does God want us to keep kosher? Some theorize that the regulations are health-based while many traditional Jews would not question the reason at all. For these Jews, the authority for all *mitzvot* is the fact that they are commanded by God; we don't need to understand God's reasons. For the rest of us, Prager and Telushkin[83] offer the following possibilities: "(1) to limit the number of animals the Jew is permitted to kill and eat, (2) to render the slaughter of the permitted animals as painless as possible, (3) to cause revulsion at the shedding of blood, (4) to instill self-discipline in the Jew, (5) to help sustain Judaism and the cohesion of the Jewish community; and (6) to raise the act of eating from an animal-like level."

My own experience with keeping *kosher* has underlined the sense of holiness associated with eating, transforming what is an animal act into a holy one. Before I eat, I reflect on God's requirements. By reciting blessings over the food, thereby thanking God, and giving thanks afterward, I acknowledge the gifts that I receive and, through the *mitzvot* system, the obligations that I have to those less fortunate. When I eat out with others, my choice of food (especially in Chinese restaurants, where we generally share food as a group) may lead to a discussion about God and Judaism, often making for a more interesting evening. Individual Jews will vary widely in their observance of *kashrut*. Many Reform Jews will not keep these laws at all, while other Jews have extended and transformed the concept to what might be called "eco-kosher," providing for use of recycled materials, products that do not make use of animal testing, and the like.

4. Blessings: At most Jewish events, you will hear one or more blessings. Each blessing, called a *bracha,* begins the same way, saying, "Blessed are You, Lord our God, King of the Universe..." (Hebrew *"Baruch Atah Adonai, Eloheinu Melech HaOlam"*). If the blessing is before eating some kind of food, it will continue to specify the food category to be eaten. The most often heard are for wine, which continues "...who creates the fruit of the vine," and for bread, which continues "...who brings forth bread from the earth." You may also hear blessings recited before performance of specific *mitzvot,* such as lighting *Shabbat* candles, which continues "...who makes us holy with His *mitzvot,* and commands us to light the *Shabbat* candles." Another common blessing is the *Sh-he-chi-yanu,* recited at holidays and important moments in an individual's or family's life

---

83. D. Prager and J. Telushkin, *The Nine Questions People Ask About Judaism,* Simon and Schuster, 1981, p. 58.

which, after the common opening, continues "…who has granted us life, sustained us, and has permitted us to reach this time."

5. Mezuzah: In the opening paragraph of the *Shema,* perhaps the best known of Jewish prayers (see discussion of liturgy above), we are told to speak the words of the prayer and laws of the Torah "when you sit in your house, when you walk by the way, when you lie down, and when you rise up.…And you shall write them upon the doorposts of your house and upon your gates" (Deut 6:7–9). Jews therefore write the words of this prayer on a small scroll and mount the scroll in a decorative cover, called a *mezuzah* (the Hebrew word for "doorpost" is *mezuzah*) on their front door (see figure 6). Jewish law in fact requires a *mezuzah* on every door of the home (or any other building), with the exception of the bathrooms and storage rooms. Traditional Jews will touch the *mezuzah* with their fingertips and then kiss them when they leave and enter a room or home.

6. Jewish Star: In the center of the flag of the State of Israel is the six-pointed star that has come to symbolize Jews and Judaism (see figure 7). The Hebrew name for the symbol is *Magen David,* meaning "shield of (King) David." Its use as a Jewish symbol is relatively recent, probably no earlier than the Middle Ages, with the most common use arising in the nineteenth century to respond to the need for a simple, easily identifiable Jewish symbol.[84] The most ancient Jewish symbol is, in fact, the seven-branched candelabrum or *menorah* that is described in the Bible (Exod 25:31–38).

7. Torah Study: For Jews, the term *Torah study* applies to the discussion and study of Jewish texts and tradition, including, but by no means limited to, the Torah (the first five books of the Bible). The Mishna teaches (tractate *Peah* 1:1) that "these are the things of which the fruits are enjoyed in this world while the capital remains for the World to Come: the honoring of parents, benevolence, restoring peace between a man and his fellow, and also the study of the Torah which is equal to them all." Most synagogues have a weekly Torah study group (often convening on Saturdays) that meets to study the Torah portion of the week or some other section of Torah or Jewish sacred literature. When Jews study our sacred literature, we only begin with the text. It is

---

84. *Encyclopaedia Judaica,* article on *Magen David,* op. cit., vol. 11, pp. 687–98.

Image copyright of SweetChild Software

Figure 6: *Mezuzah and Scroll*

Image copyright of SweetChild Software

Figure 7: *Jewish Star on Israeli Flag*

very important to have available the commentaries of the great rabbis and other scholars so that our own study can benefit from their insights. Christians are generally welcome at such study, and you will be surprised and interested to learn of the depth of commentary and insight available to you through Jewish texts and commentaries. It's important to understand that for Jews, study is its own reward. Rabbi Elijah of Vilna, a renowned scholar, was quoted as saying, "If an angel were to offer me all the knowledge of the Torah at once, I would not accept it. For study, not knowledge, is the chief thing."[85]

8. Tzedakah: Although this word is usually translated as "charity," its literal meaning is "justice" or "righteousness." Giving money to appropriate causes is not considered just a good deed that comes from the heart, but an act of justice. The converse is also true: failing to give an appropriate amount (10 percent, according to the Talmud), is an act of injustice. The idea is that this portion of your funds does not in fact belong to you; God has merely entrusted it to you to disburse appropriately.

ODDS AND ENDS

1. Tikkun Olam—Repair of the World: God could have created the world perfect and complete—no disease, no war, no hunger, no problems even as minor as dandruff! But think about it—if this were the case, what would our job be? What would be the reason for our existence? Judaism holds that one of its primary tasks is to work on the world's problems and solve them. Thus we concern ourselves with issues as diverse as hunger, disease, war, education, and the environment. In this way, we are God's partners in bringing creation toward its intended goal. The Hebrew phrase that captures this task is *tikkun olam,* meaning repair or completion of the world.

2. Conversion and Who Is a Jew: There are two ways to become Jewish: by birth or by conversion. For Orthodox and Conservative Jews, a person is born a Jew if he or she has a Jewish mother. Their Jewish status is a matter of birth and not of belief. Even if a born Jew were to actively disavow the existence of God, any child of a Jewish

85. Wylen, *Settings of Silver,* op. cit., p. 20.

mother would still be considered fully Jewish. Such a child is considered by Judaism to be 100 percent Jewish whereas a child of a Jewish father and a non-Jewish mother is traditionally considered to be a non-Jew. There are no 50 percent Jews. The Reform and Reconstructionist movements provide for "patrilineal descent," which allows for a child of only one Jewish parent, mother or father, to be considered a Jew so long as the child is raised with public and formal acts of Jewish identification (including circumcision, Hebrew naming, receiving a Jewish education, *Bar/Bat Mitzvah,* etc.).

For the past two thousand years, Jews have not actively sought converts since seeking or being converted to Judaism was often considered a capital crime. Today, anyone interested in converting to Judaism should contact a rabbi, who will provide for a course of study. With the study requirements completed, all Orthodox and Conservative, and many Reconstructionist and Reform rabbis, would require immersion in a ritual bath *(mikveh)* for both men and women and circumcision for men (men already circumcised would have a symbolic drop of blood drawn in a religious ceremony). The convert is then asked whether he takes on the *mitzvot* of Judaism and renounces all prior religious beliefs. Once welcomed into the community of Judaism, the "Jew by Choice" (a term often preferred over *convert*) is fully Jewish; the Talmud forbids us to remind someone that she is a convert.

3. Intermarriage: One consequence of the acceptance of Jews by the larger non-Jewish community is the tremendous increase in intermarriage, or interfaith marriage. Today, between a third and a half of marriages involving a Jew is an intermarriage, a rate some ten times greater than that before the 1960s. The high rate of intermarriage is of great concern to the Jewish community since it is not unusual for the children of such marriages not to identify themselves as Jews when they become adults. The Reform movement has been especially active in "outreach" to intermarried couples to help resolve conflicts, to address the "December Dilemma" (the conflicts that arise during the Christmas–*Hanukkah* season), and to support those couples who want to raise their children as Jews.

As Jewish law forbids intermarriage, most rabbis will not preside at such ceremonies. The most significant exception to this rule is that many (just under half) Reform and Reconstructionist rabbis will conduct a Jewish wedding between Jew and non-Jew provided that the promises of the wedding, especially that of creating a Jewish home, are taken seriously. Such rabbis will commonly require that the non-Jewish spouse take a course in order to better understand Judaism. Only a tiny fraction of such rabbis will agree to co-officiate at a wedding with non-Jewish clergy.

4. Languages—Hebrew: The Hebrew language is the only language ever to fall into disuse and to be later revived.[86] The Jewish Bible, Mishna, and prayerbook are all written in Hebrew but, with the destruction of the Temple and the dispersion of Jews, the language fell into disuse as a spoken tongue. It continued to be used for prayer, study of sacred texts, poetry, *responsa,* and international Jewish correspondence. The revival of the language can be largely attributed to Eliezer Ben-Yehuda (1858–1922), who believed that the Jews of Israel must speak this language to unite them. He insisted on speaking Hebrew at home, and created a modern Hebrew dictionary by formulating thousands of words that did not exist in biblical days.

Hebrew has its own alphabet and is written from right to left. North American Jewish children receiving their training for *Bar/Bat Mitzvah* are taught how to read Hebrew and how to chant Hebrew prayers, generally beginning their instruction at age six or younger. Immigrants arriving in Israel are given six months or more of intensive training in Hebrew since the language is in fact the one spoken on the streets.

5. Languages—Yiddish and Ladino: Over the centuries in which Hebrew was used largely for prayer, Jewish folk languages developed. For the Eastern European Ashkenazi Jews, the language was Yiddish, a mixture of Hebrew and German (as well as small amounts of other local languages such as Polish, Russian, Lithuanian, etc.) written with Hebrew characters. Hasidic Jews today still speak Yiddish, preferring not to use Hebrew for anything but prayer and study. Many Yiddish words such as *klutz, chutzpa, nosh, schmooze,* and *shlep* (see the glossary for definitions) have made it into English parlance.[87] The Sephardic parallel to Yiddish is Ladino, a mixture of Spanish and Hebrew with some local Turkish, Italian, French, Greek, and Arabic thrown in. Since

---

86. Ibid., p. 322.
87. Well-documented in Leo Rosten's *The Joys of Yinglish,* McGraw-Hill, 1989.

the Jewish immigration to North America was far more Ashkenazi than Sephardic, Yiddish is much better known here.

6. *Mysticism and Kabbalah:* With Judaism's emphasis on law and study, one might be tempted to think that there is not much room for mysticism. Happily, this is not the case. Throughout the centuries, there has always been a strong sense of the mystical in Judaism. Jewish mystical studies are called *kabbalah* (meaning "received tradition") and a primary goal of Jewish mysticism is to understand the nature of God and come closer to God (to the point of spiritual unification). The primary text of *kabbalah* is the *Zohar,* a book scholars believe was written in the thirteenth century by Spanish Jews. (Traditionally, the author of the *Zohar,* the "Book of Splendors," was held to be Rabbi Simeon bar Yohai, a second-century C.E. rabbi; the book was said to be lost for all of the intervening centuries.) The book itself is a commentary on the Torah that points to a unique aspect of Jewish spirituality. As my teacher, Rabbi Lawrence Kushner, stresses, Jewish spirituality almost always starts with a sacred text as a beginning.

A complete discussion of mysticism is well beyond the scope of this "nutshell."[88] I should note that a wide range of teachings is addressed in *kabbalah,* including reincarnation, astrology, and meditation. Many *kabbalistic* teachings and prayers have made it into modern Jewish practice and the prayerbook, adding a wonderful flavor. Hasidic practice is particularly rich in mystical thought and observance, and a revival of interest in *kabbalah* is increasingly seen in the various Jewish movements, especially in a new group in Judaism that calls itself "Jewish Renewal." One interesting and important mystical idea is that each time a Jew performs a *mitzvah* or commandment of God, she contributes to the repair or perfection of the world (Hebrew *tikkun olam*). This is said to be true of the ritual *mitzvot* as well as the ethical ones.

7. *Superstition, Stereotypes, and Myths:* The long history of antisemitism has given rise to a wide range of superstitions and myths about Jews. Jews may be thought of as cheap, rich, shrewd, controlling of various industries (movies, banking, stocks and bonds, etc.), secretive, racist, or having horns, to name but a few. It is not my purpose to

---

88. An excellent introduction is given in *Settings of Silver,* op. cit.

refute these, only to make you aware of them. Almost any broad generality you might say about "all Jews" is sure to be wrong; as we saw earlier, you cannot even say that all Jews believe in God! In some cases, specific myths can be traced. For example, the idea that Jews have horns stems from a misreading of the Hebrew word *karan,* meaning "radiant," as *keren,* meaning "horned" in the description of Moses when he came down from Mt. Sinai the second time (Exod 34:29–30— such errors are understandable since the original text has no vowels that would distinguish between the two words). This error resulted in Michelangelo's famous statue of Moses with apparent horns. Other myths, such as those relating to Jews and money, have their origins in the fact that the role of money lender was the only one allowed to many Jews by the authorities in the Middle Ages. Large numbers of Jews have suffered considerably as a result of the spreading of these myths.

8. *Jewish Humor:* Our special relationship with God, our long-suffering status as outsiders in virtually every culture in which we have lived, and our love of life seem to have contributed to the rich literature of Jewish humor. There are many interesting and entertaining books on Jewish humor (see the bibliography) that seek to explain the phenomenon as well as the fact that so many comedians on the American and world stage were and are Jewish. While there is no completely common characteristic to all of Jewish humor, it seems to me that it is generally a form of humor that is self-deprecating, not mean-spirited, and just as likely to evoke a tear as a chuckle. Underlying Jewish humor is a bit of the tension of not quite belonging yet wanting to feel like an insider. Perhaps Groucho Marx said it best when he quipped that he would never want to belong to a club that would accept him as a member.

* * *

I hope that these "nutshells" have served to whet your appetite about Judaism and Jewish practice. You will find more information about each of these items in any of the many introduction to Judaism books listed in the bibliography. One of these books, *Jewish Literacy* by Joseph Telushkin, actually contains 346 brief chapters of a page or two in length covering these and many other topics. Beyond this, you can without a doubt find whole books and series of books on each of the topics highlighted above. The limits are only that of your time and access to a Jewish library (to be found at any synagogue).

Perhaps the best story of "Judaism in a nutshell" involves the sage, Hillel who lived during the time of Jesus. The Talmud (*Shabbat* 31a) relates a story of a non-Jew who asks Hillel to teach him the entire Torah while he (the non-Jew) stands on one foot. Rather than chasing him away as another sage had done, Hillel responds, "What is hateful unto you do not do unto your neighbor, the rest is commentary—now go and study." I wish you happy reading and happy study in your pursuit of Jewish knowledge!

8
Your Guide to Attending Jewish Events

So, you've been invited to a Jewish wedding, a *Bar* or *Bat Mitzvah,* a *Shabbat* (Sabbath) dinner, a Passover *Seder,* or other celebration and you don't know what to expect. How should I dress? What should I bring? What's going to happen? How can I avoid being embarrassed? Will they speak English? Will I have to do anything strange? You don't quite know what you're getting into and, despite the best assurances of the folks that have invited you, you're nervous and insecure. This chapter is for you!

A disclaimer and word of warning. There is much variation in Jewish practice, even within a specific movement such as Reform or Conservative Judaism, so that no one single guide can describe every possible custom that you might see in a specific event. Moreover, it is not the goal of this brief chapter to provide a complete background and description of each of the events presented. The chapter covers the major elements of each, and the most common variations that you're likely to see. I hope the descriptions will boost your courage and help you enjoy your participation in what is probably a very important event in the life of someone you care deeply about. Enjoy!

One more item. If you're reading this book straight through, you will notice that I cover many of the same items in this chapter that I did in the previous one. My intent is to have this chapter be able to stand on its own so you can find out what you need to know if, say, you're going to a Passover *Seder,* without having to check back through the previous chapters. That means that there will be some repetition of material I've covered previously.

A JEWISH RELIGIOUS SERVICE

You won't be surprised to learn that many Jewish celebrations revolve around a religious service. Each religious service follows a prescribed order of prayers and activities assembled in the Jewish prayerbook (Hebrew *Siddur*). The prayerbooks of the Orthodox and Conservative movements are quite different from each other and from those of the Reform movement. In general, you'll find that a Reform service has much more English than a Conservative service, which, in turn, has more than an Orthodox service. In addition, the Reform service is likely to be the shortest, with Conservative and Orthodox following in increasing length.

When: Traditional Jews pray three services a day with the afternoon and evening service usually combined, so you could be attending a service at almost any time. Most likely, you will be going to a *Shabbat* service either Friday night (just after sundown at traditional synagogues or often at a fixed time, say 8:00 P.M., at a Reform or Conservative synagogue) or Saturday morning (starting at a fixed time, usually from 9:00 to 11:00 A.M.). Occasionally, you may be invited to a *Shabbat Mincha* service, sometimes called a *Havdalah* service, which will take place late Saturday afternoon.

Who Will Be There: The officiants are likely to be a rabbi and a cantor (see chapter 7 for a discussion of their roles), although it is not unusual for a service to have no cantor and even to have no rabbi; such a service would be led by a knowledgeable congregant or even a rabbinic student. In most cases, there will be a wide variety of attendees (young, old, couples, singles, etc.) from the congregational community.

Where Will It Be Held: The usual location is a synagogue but a small worship service might also take place in someone's home. It's also not uncommon for smaller congregations to hold services in a church, school building, or other convenient location.

What's Going to Happen: It is customary (especially in Orthodox and Conservative congregations) for attending men and boys to cover their heads with skullcaps (Hebrew *kippah;* Yiddish *yarmulke*), and, at morning service to wear the traditional prayer shawl (Hebrew *tallit;* Yiddish *tallis*). Non-Jewish men should cover their heads at Orthodox and Conservative services but should not wear a prayer shawl. In most Orthodox congregations (but rarely in Conservative and never in Reform ones), men and women will be seated separately (this tradition seeks to promote better concentration on the service). Everyone will be praying from the prayerbook *(Siddur)* that is provided. You will also notice that a copy of the Torah (a book containing the first five books of the Bible along with commentaries and associated sections from the books of the Prophets—this is sometimes titled the *Pentateuch* or a *Chumash*) is available for those services in which the Torah is read. The rabbi or leader will, from time to time, announce what page the congregation is on as well as when to stand and when to sit. Just try to follow along and don't be shy about asking your neighbor about "what page we're on." You may read and pray with the congregation (in the English sections or even in the Hebrew—sometimes there is transliteration of the most important Hebrew prayers) or just remain silent. You may stand and sit with the congregation or remain seated. There is no point in the service when congregants are asked to kneel. The standard of service decorum will vary greatly, from the formal behavior and responsive readings common in Reform congregations, to an interesting mixture of different people chanting or reading silently at different paces and even talking to one another in more traditional congregations. By observing the congregation, you should be able to pick up cues quickly.

Even if you are not familiar with the prayers, you will notice that there is a great deal of attention paid to the holy ark (Hebrew *aron kodesh*) at the front of the synagogue. The ark contains the Torah scrolls that belong to the synagogue (see chapter 7 for more on the Torah). If you are at a Torah service (every Monday, Thursday, and Saturday, and major holidays, also Friday nights in some Reform congregations), a scroll will be taken from the ark, carried around the congregation (symbolizing the moment that Moses brought the Torah to the entire people of Israel), and the congregants will typically touch their hand or a book to the Torah and then kiss the hand or book. This and other activities, such as standing when the ark is open and bowing to the ark during a number of prayers, indicate the great respect we Jews have for the Torah. You may or may not wish to join in paying this respect to the Torah; there's no problem either way.

At the conclusion of the service, especially if it is a Sabbath service, there will often be some refreshments (often called an *Oneg,* which means "delight"; the Bible—Isa 58:13—tells us to call the Sabbath a delight). These will typically be preceded by a blessing called a *bracha,* which praises God as the Sovereign of the universe and thanks God for the specific food that is given (usually bread and/or wine); wait until after the blessing before eating. Eating these foods does not have the ritual or symbolic implications as does taking communion in many Christian churches (although it is the origin of these Christian practices); thus you may feel free to partake or not (you're just eating wine and bread and nothing more). By the way, by responding "amen" to the *bracha* (or for any other prayer for that matter), Judaism holds it exactly as if you had joined in the recitation. At the conclusion of the service, the congregants will typically greet each other (saying, *"Shabbat shalom,"* meaning "Sabbath greetings" or "a peaceful Sabbath"; the Yiddish equivalent is *"gut Shabbos,"* meaning "good Sabbath") and then chat for some time.

By the way, you will *never* see a collection plate passed at a Jewish Sabbath or holiday service since carrying or handling money on these days is traditionally forbidden. Should you wish to make a donation to the synagogue, you should send one in later by mail (and not on the Sabbath itself).

Do's and Don'ts: Do ask your hosts about expected dress before coming; this is a matter of custom at each synagogue, but often calls for your "Sunday best" out of respect for the holiness of the day. You should expect to use good decorum as you would in a church service. Ask your hosts what the local custom is regarding attendance of small children. You may find that a special program will be provided for them. You may generally sit wherever you please (remembering that at Orthodox services men and women sit separately). Don't enter or exit the sanctuary when the congregation is standing. If you are at a Sabbath or holiday service, you should not take photographs or video-tape the service unless you have specific approval in advance. Smoking on the Sabbath is generally frowned upon.

BAR OR BAT MITZVAH

The words *Bar/Bat Mitzvah* mean "Son/Daughter of Commandment." Your invitation may be to a *Bas Mitzvah* (*Bas* is the Yiddish/Ashkenazi pronunciation of *Bat*). The ceremony to which you have been invited is held in honor of the child reaching the age of majority under Jewish law. This is traditionally twelve years of age for a girl and thirteen years for a boy (yes, Judaism recognizes that girls mature sooner), and means that the child is now responsible for observing Jewish law. One privilege of Jewish law is that an adult Jew may lead a religious service and be called to read from the Torah scroll. When you attend a *Bar/Bat Mitzvah,* you are attending the religious service at which the child will lead some part (or even all) of the services as well as read from the Torah scroll.

Regarding Jewish students older than thirteen, there are two more recent developments. The Reform movement introduced the idea of a Confirmation ceremony for sixteen-year-old students. This ceremony, which usually takes place on the holiday of *Shavuot,* is a group graduation of those boys and girls who have continued their studies past *Bar/Bat Mitzvah* age. You may also be invited to the *Bar/Bat Mitzvah* of an adult. Increasingly, adult Jews mark their recommitment to Jewish life and study with such a ceremony, especially if they never formally became a *Bar/Bat Mitzvah* as children.

When: The vast majority of *B'nai Mitzvah* (*B'nai* is the plural) take place on *Shabbat,* that is, Friday nights and Saturdays. Technically, it is possible to hold a *Bar/Bat Mitzvah* on any day in which the Torah is read from the scroll. This would include Mondays and Thursdays (traditional market days in ancient times) as well as certain Jewish holidays.

Who Will Be There: Since this will most often be a standard Sabbath service, in addition to the friends and family of the child, you are likely to find other members of the congregation. Remember, the synagogue portion of the *Bar/Bat Mitzvah* is not a private party but part of a community worship service.

Where It Will Be Held: In most cases, at the synagogue. Occasionally, a catering hall or other location may be the site for the ceremony and reception.

What's Going to Happen: This will be a standard Sabbath service with particular opportunities for recognition of the child and his or her family. You will notice special, often moving, moments when the family presents the child with his or her *tallit,* or prayer shawl, and when the rabbi and other members of the congregation (often including the child's parents) are called upon to bless, congratulate, and speak to the child. The child may conduct some or all of the service but will almost certainly be called to read or chant from the Torah scroll itself and read or chant from the prophetic section *(haftarah)* of the Hebrew Bible. The portion of the scripture the child is reading is the specific *parasha,* or portion of the week, and this same portion is also being read in synagogues throughout the world. Typically, members of the child's family and friends will be called to the reading table to say blessings at the Torah and watch while the rabbi or cantor and child read from the Torah scroll. Being called to the Torah is an *aliyah* (meaning "going up") and is among the greatest of honors. This honor is usually restricted to Jews since the blessing recited speaks of God's having "chosen *us*" and "given *us*" (that is, the Jewish people) the Torah. It is very common for the child to deliver a sermon after having read the Torah and *haftarah* sections. In this way, the child is fulfilling the *mitzvah* (commandment) of teaching our tradition.

After the service, it is quite common to have a reception for the child and her or his family (you will be invited). The reception may be as simple as coffee and treats at the synagogue or may be a very elaborate catered affair held at the synagogue or at another location.

Do's and Don'ts: The do's and don'ts relating to attendance at Jewish services (see above) apply here since you will be attending a Jewish service. I would recommend that you not bring any gift to the service itself, but save it for the reception. Regarding gift giving, it is common to present a check or savings bond to the child. If you want to give a monetary gift that has a special significance, you might give a gift involving the number 18 or a multiple of 18, such as $36 or $118. Hebrew letters each have numerical equivalents and the Hebrew word *chai,* meaning "life," has the value of 18. Sephardic Jews will commonly give gifts in multiples of 5—an association with the five fingers of the *hamsa,* or hand of God that protects us. A personal gift chosen in consultation with the family would also be very appreciated: it might be a book or religious article of Jewish significance.

VISITING SOMEONE'S HOME ON *SHABBAT* EVENING

One answer to the question "Do Jews miss celebrating such Christian holidays as Christmas and Easter?" is that we have a wonderful holiday every week—the Sabbath (Hebrew *Shabbat;* Yiddish *Shabbos*). There are a great many laws about what one is permitted to do (or is forbidden to do) on the Sabbath. While at first glance they appear to be quite restrictive, closer examination reveals their true intent: to liberate us from the day-to-day tedium of ordinary life in order to have a day of rest, relaxation, and celebration. The mystics believe that *Shabbat* is a taste of the world to come, the world redeemed in messianic times.[89] We don't shop for anything because we are imagining that we don't need anything. We don't work because there is no work to do! We've completed it all (an echo of God's completion of His work of creation) and for that day, the world is perfect. What is left to do? Enjoy meals, sing, visit friends and family, worship together, nap, and study (for the joy of studying—not for exams and/or business).

When: The most common invitation is likely to be to a Sabbath dinner, held Friday night. In traditional homes, Sabbath candles are lit eighteen minutes before sundown, after which the family (sometimes just the men) attends a brief *Erev Shabbat* (Sabbath Evening) service. After the service, the family and guests return home for the *Shabbat* meal. In Reform and Conservative practice, the meal may precede services that might begin as late as 8:00 or 8:30 P.M. You may find that your hosts may be holding a Sabbath meal and have no plans to attend services at all. You may or may not be invited to attend services; feel free to ask if the family is attending services and if you can come along.

Who Will Be There: This clearly depends on your hosts. You may find that only your hosts and the immediate family are present or you may find friends, neighbors, and even strangers present (hospitality to strangers is a major *mitzvah* for Jews, especially on *Shabbat*).

Where It Will Be Held: Almost certainly at the home of your hosts (and not, for example, at a restaurant).

What's Going to Happen: Expect a period of greeting and chatting (Yiddish *schmoozing*) before getting down to the more formal

---

89. Greenberg, *The Jewish Way,* op. cit., p. 128.

elements of the dinner. The woman of the house and, perhaps, her daughters will light the Sabbath candles if they have not been lit yet (traditionally, men light Sabbath candles only if women are not present). There will probably be two candles, representing the twin commandments to "remember" (Exod 20:8) and "observe" (Deut 5:12) the Sabbath. After this, it is traditional for parents to bless their children and, in some households, for people to bless each other. Try it, you'll love it! You may want to make such blessings part of your own Sabbath traditions.

When everyone has been seated at the Sabbath table, customarily set with the family's finest linens, glassware, and silverware, the leader (traditionally the male head of household but commonly others) will lead the group in the *kiddush,* a prayer that blesses the Sabbath through the symbol of wine (sweet wine or grape juice is used to symbolize the sweetness of life). The wine glass may be passed for each participant to sip or you may have the *kiddush* wine in your own cup. In either case, the wine is not a sacrament; it's just wine and you may drink it without compromising your religious beliefs.

In more traditional homes, the *kiddush* will be followed by a ritual washing of hands (this is a cleansing for spiritual purity—it is presumed that hygienic cleansing has already taken place). Often silence will be maintained until the *challah,* the traditional braided loaf of bread for the Sabbath, is blessed and eaten. Traditionally there are two loaves in memory of the double portion of *manna* in the desert provided to the Hebrews every Friday (Exod 16:5). Note that the *challah* has been kept covered both as a reminder of the dew that covered the *manna* and out of respect for the *challah*'s feelings while the wine is being blessed. (A wonderful Hasidic story teaches that if we go so far to respect the feelings of loaves of bread, how much further should we go to respect people's sensitivities.) After the blessing, pieces of the *challah* may be salted (relating back to practices at the Temple—see Lev 2:13), distributed, and eaten. Once again, feel free to partake of this wonderful braided egg bread.

Each family will have its own traditions and discussion topics for the meal. Some may discuss something to be happy or grateful about in the week that has passed. Some families may discuss the Torah portion of the week or another Jewish text. The goal is to lift the discussion above everyday topics. Dinner discussion is a perfect time for you to ask any questions you might have about Judaism or Jewish practice. Dinner will often be followed by singing and stories, and concluded with the *Birkat Hamazon,* or the blessing after meals. This is a somewhat lengthy prayer that is chanted as a group to a wide variety of melodies (once, in Jerusalem, I heard a portion of this prayer sung to "It's a Small World After All").

Do's and Don'ts: The easiest thing to bring to the dinner is a bouquet of flowers. It's best to avoid bringing any food items, lest they be incompatible with the family's dietary practices. Also check with your hosts about what to wear; *Shabbat* dinner may be dressier than you might think. In accepting your invitation, make sure it's on a day that you don't have to "eat and run." You should come expecting a leisurely evening of food, discussion, laughter, and song. Worrying about the time is definitely not in the *Shabbat* spirit. By the way, the greeting upon entering and leaving the home is Hebrew *"Shabbat shalom!"* and Yiddish *"gut Shabbos!"*

VISITING SOMEONE'S HOME FOR A PASSOVER *SEDER*

Mazel tov (congratulations)! You are in for a treat, having been invited to attend a *Pesach* (Passover) *Seder.* The *Seder* is a ritual meal held on the first and sometimes the second evenings of the holiday (see chapter 7 for a discussion of Passover). The word *Seder* literally means "order" in Hebrew, a reference to the carefully prescribed order of events that will occur this evening. The overall purpose of the evening is to commemorate the exodus of the Jews from Egypt some 3,200 years ago and, further, to remember the evening in which the angel of God "passed over" the homes of the Israelites to claim only the firstborn of Egypt. The Torah (Exod 12:16) requires us to hold a "sacred convocation" in memory of the event. But, as you will see, we do more than just remember. We are instructed to imagine and feel as though each of us were slaves in Egypt and we ourselves were freed. As Rabbi Irving Greenberg put it: "one must be a bit of a ham to be a kosher Jew."[90] Another objective of the evening is to arouse and hold the interest of the children present so they will want to know more about the exodus, the central event in our salvation history and a key metaphor for the deliverance from all that enslaves us.

---

90. Ibid., p. 13.

When: Many Jews observe two Passover *Seder*s on successive nights, even though the Reform movement officially does not require the second. Commonly, congregations will hold a community *Seder* on the second night; you might want to attend one of these even if you've not been invited to another. Call the synagogue and check on availability (such *Seder*s are often advertised in local newspapers and certainly in Jewish newspapers and non-Jews are generally welcome). The first night of the holiday falls on the evening of the fourteenth day of the Hebrew month of *Nissan*. This means that it will fall anywhere from late March until mid-April on our secular calendars. Be sure to check with your hosts about the start time of the *Seder* since you do not want to hold up or miss any of the proceedings.

Who Will Be There: While the *Seder* you attend may be an intimate affair with just the immediate family, it is more common to find that every spare bit of floor space anywhere in the vicinity of the kitchen or dining room (or other rooms throughout the house) has been transformed into an eating area. Some of my earliest and most wonderful memories are evenings spent in crowded homes and apartments with distant cousins whom I only saw once a year, going through the ritual and searching for the hidden *afikomen* (see below). So don't be surprised to find a combination of family, friends, business associates, and even strangers at the table. Attendance at a *Pesach Seder* is the most observed Jewish ritual in the United States; you will not be lonely tonight.

Where It Will Be Held: While the most likely locale for the *Seder* is at your hosts' home, you may even find that they have rented a large room somewhere to accommodate the throngs of people attending.

What's Going to Happen: As noted above, the very word *Seder* indicates that there is to be a specified order to the events of the evening. To preserve this "order," there is a specific prayerbook that has evolved called the *Haggadah*. It has been estimated that there have been more than two thousand different editions of the *Haggadah* printed[91] and, at most *Seder*s that I've attended, more than one version has been used. The *Haggadah* serves as the script for the evening. It lists the fifteen traditional steps for the *Seder* and presents the text to be

---

91. Joseph Telushkin, *Jewish Literacy*, William Morrow, 1991, p. 584.

Figure 8: A Seder Plate

read and sung. It also offers stage directions such as when to wash hands, when to break the *matzah* (see figure 4), and when to eat the meal. The *Haggadah* may be very traditional, with lots of Hebrew, or it may be quite contemporary; it might also be designed to involve the children. You will probably find a *Haggadah* at your plate. Open it and browse a bit before the formal proceedings get started (you might even want to ask your hosts if you can borrow one to examine before coming—or you might even want to purchase an inexpensive *Haggadah* for your own education). The first thing you'll note is that often the beginning of the book is where you'd expect to find the end. Remember, Hebrew is read from right to left and Hebrew books also open the "wrong way." The *Haggadah* in your hands may be beautifully illustrated, with scenes from the biblical story and from the *Seder* table itself.

Let's discuss the *Seder* plate in the center of the table(s) and traditional foods on the plates (see figure 8):

- A roasted bone: this is a remembrance of the sacrifice of the Pascal lamb offered on Passover in biblical times at the Temple in Jerusalem.
- A roasted egg: this also recalls a special festival sacrifice offered on Passover.

- Greens (such as parsley): a symbol of the springtime season in which the holiday falls.
- *Maror* (or bitter herbs): recalling the bitterness of slavery.
- *Haroset* (a mixture of several ingredients): designed to remind us of the mortar the Hebrews used to build Pharaoh's monuments.
- A dish of salt water: recalling the tears of slaves.
- Three pieces of *matzah: matzah* (see figure 4), or unleavened bread, is both the bread of slavery (a poor, simple bread that is inexpensive and yet filling) and the bread of freedom (flat, since the Hebrews, fearing Pharaoh would change his mind about their freedom, did not have time to let their bread rise once freedom was granted). Jewish law requires that we eat only *matzah* on this night and on all of the days of *Pesach;* during this period, we are forbidden to eat *chometz,* or leavened bread.
- A large wine cup (the Cup of Elijah): attendees drink four cups of wine during the *Seder,* corresponding to the four terms the Bible uses for redemption in Exodus 6:6–7. The rabbis could not decide if a later promise (in Exod 6:8) should prompt a fifth cup of wine, so they decided to leave one in the hopes that the prophet Elijah would appear and make a final decision on the matter.

The leader of the *Seder* will call the group to order and begin the readings from the *Haggadah.* In many *Seder*s I've attended, we went around the room taking turns reading the English so that everyone has a part to play. Although the amount of Hebrew used will vary at the discretion of the leader, you will almost always hear Hebrew blessings for the ritual foods and a Hebrew recitation of the beloved "Four Questions." The questions ask: "Why is this night different from all other nights? Why do we eat *matzah* and not *chometz?* Why do we eat bitter herbs? Why do we dip our herbs twice? Why do we eat reclining on pillows?" The questions are traditionally asked by the youngest child present that is able to ask. Sometimes all the children will chant the questions together as their parents beam with pride. The goal is to involve the children. But it should also be a signal to you. After checking with your hosts, you should feel free to ask your own questions, perhaps during the ritual proceeding itself, but certainly during the meal. As a non-Jew, you will be able to ask the questions that some of the Jews present would like to ask but may feel embarrassed to do so. You may find that there are lots of different answers to your questions. It all adds to the fun and supports the objectives of the evening.

The highlights of the *Seder* (at least for me) are:

- The asking of the "Four Questions."
- Eating the ritual foods such as *matzah,* bitter herbs, the leafy vegetable, and the *haroset,* and drinking the wine.
- The symbolic spilling of wine during the recitation of the plagues. As we name each of the ten plagues sent against the Egyptians, we remove a little wine from our cups. This diminution of our "full cup of joy" is in recognition of the fact that Egyptians (also God's children) had to die in the process of redemption from slavery.
- Opening the door for Elijah the prophet who, we hope, will arrive to settle the question of the fifth cup of wine (see above) and usher in the Messianic Age.
- The hiding and finding of the *afikomen,* a bit of *matzah* needed to complete the meal. This "hide and seek" game is yet another ploy to keep the children involved.
- The meal itself.
- Singing traditional songs after the meal.

It's hard for me to prepare you any further for the events of the evening since *Seder*s take on the character of the hosts and the group assembled. But just relax and enjoy. Short of asking "Isn't there any bread?" (see do's and don'ts below), there's not much you can do that's wrong.

Do's and Don'ts: The prohibition against eating (or even owning) anything leavened means that there is a special set of kosher rules for the Passover holiday. The rules are so strict that traditional Jews keep a separate set of dishes, silverware, and even pots and pans for use during this holiday. Even Jews who are not at all observant of the kosher laws throughout the year may keep the kosher rules for *Pesach* during the *Seder* itself. So, to be on the safe side, don't bring any food items to the dinner. Once again, ask your hosts for specific advice as to what you may bring (you may find that you'll be asked to bring folding chairs and tables). As in the case of the Sabbath dinner, flowers are always appropriate and safe. Try to arrive on time and don't come starving since the ritual takes a bit of time (usually not less than an hour) before the meal begins. On the other hand, you will find that the meal will be more than ample; you will not leave hungry.

The appropriate greeting for this holiday is the generic Hebrew *chag sah-may-ach* ("happy holiday") or Yiddish *gut yontif* ("good holiday").

A final note on the *Seder*'s significance to Christians. It is generally thought that Jesus' Last Supper was a Passover *Seder*. The communion of a wafer and wine that many Christians use in their services is a direct link to this holiday. On a spiritual level, it is easy to see the connection between the spiritual redemption from sin that Christians find in the Easter holiday season and the physical and spiritual freedom that Jews celebrate at *Pesach*.

A CIRCUMCISION (*BRIS*, OR *BRIT MILAH*) AND/OR BABY-NAMING

The reason for circumcision is very clear: the Torah (Gen 17:9–14, 24–25) quotes God as commanding Abraham to circumcise himself (at age ninety nine!), his son Ishmael (then thirteen), and all the males in his household (including his slaves). Children born thereafter are to be circumcised at the age of eight days. Circumcision is identified as the "sign of the covenant" between God and the Jewish people. The Hebrew word for circumcision is *milah,* the Hebrew word for covenant is *brit* (Yiddish *bris*), and the act of circumcision is called a *Brit (Bris) Milah* or, quite commonly among American Jews (of Ashkenazi origin), a *Bris.* Jews throughout the centuries have clung to this ritual even during those times when circumcision exposed the parents and child to mortal danger. Much has been written about the underlying reasons for, as well as the alleged benefits and dangers of, circumcision. Jews, however, circumcise their baby boys not for medical reasons; *Milah* is a symbol of the covenant between God and the Jewish people. My favorite interpretation of this ritual is that it symbolizes the fact that God did not perfect creation (in this case, creation of a person). It is up to us to complete creation of this baby and of the world. Since the protection and preservation of life is the highest value in Judaism, children for whom circumcision would be dangerous (hemophiliacs, for example) are not circumcised. Similarly, if the child has a temporary medical condition counterindicating circumcision, the *Brit Milah* will be delayed until it is safe to perform. Boys and men of all ages converting to Judaism are circumcised, or if already circumcised, have a symbolic drop of blood drawn.

It is traditional for the child to be given a Hebrew name at the circumcision ceremony. If the boy has been circumcised in the hospital, or if the celebration is for a baby girl, the ceremony may be a "Baby-Naming" only. Traditionally, baby girls are named in the synagogue at the first Torah reading or *Shabbat* after their birth. More and more frequently, however, moving and beautiful rituals for the Baby-Naming have been developed that welcome both boys and girls into the covenant of Abraham and Sarah. These rituals are often conducted at home. Among Ashkenazi families, it is customary to name the child after a beloved dead relative. The origin of the child's Hebrew name will be explained at the ceremony.

When: The Torah commands that circumcision take place on the eighth day of the boy's life. Some say this is so the child will have been through at least one Sabbath, others say that this is the time when the child is medically most able to tolerate the procedure. The commandment to circumcise on the eighth day is so strong that the *Brit Milah* will take place on the eighth day even if it falls on *Shabbat* or *Yom Kippur.* So, if the circumcision is on Tuesday morning, your hosts are not being inconsiderate of schedules, but observant of tradition's schedule. More recently, it has become the practice of less observant Jews to have the *Brit* on a day more convenient for family and friends to attend, or to have the actual circumcision performed in the hospital either with or without the Jewish rituals. A Baby-Naming then takes place later (sometimes months later) at a more convenient time.

Who Will Be There: For both a *Brit Milah* and Baby-Naming, you can expect that friends and family will be well represented. Although the actual obligation to circumcise the baby boy falls to the child's father, I am happy (as both a father of a boy and as a rabbi) to tell you that a specialist in the ritual and medical aspects of circumcision, the *mohel* (Yiddish *moyel*) actually performs the procedure. In the case of a Baby-Naming, a rabbi will often preside.

Where It Will Be Held: Most often the circumcision will be at the child's home, but sometimes it will be at a synagogue or hospital.

What's Going to Happen: In the case of a circumcision, the *mohel* (or rabbi if a physician is performing the actual procedure) will often begin by explaining the origins of circumcision. The child will be brought into the room and held by his godparents. You may also notice a special chair designated as Elijah's Chair. Elijah's name is invoked for at least two reasons: (1) the prophet is understood to be the precursor of the Messiah, and, who knows, maybe this baby is the Messiah; and (2) since he lost faith in Israel's future at one point, Elijah has been commanded to be present at all future circumcisions to witness the continued loyalty of Jews to the covenant. The child's father may be asked by the *mohel* if he would like to perform the circumcision himself or allow the *mohel* to do it for him (I've never heard of a case in which the father wanted to step in). Both parents may read prayers relating to the ritual.

The child is secured onto a table that looks like a car seat designed to prevent him from moving during the procedure. He is given a gauze strip or a finger dipped in a bit of wine; this often seems to distract him. His foreskin is pulled free of the glans of the penis and clamped (there are several different types of clamps) so that the scalpel cannot inadvertently harm the penis itself. If there's room around the baby, it's perfectly okay for you to watch the procedure. If you blink, you may miss it. Just before the circumcision, the father or parents recite the blessing relating to the commandment for circumcision. Afterward, everyone shouts *"mazel tov"* (congratulations) and breathes a great sigh of relief. The ritual designating the boy's name follows, along with a sumptuous (usually dairy—symbolizing life) meal. Baby-Naming ceremonies for boys and girls include many of these same elements with the exception, of course, of the circumcision itself.

Do's and Don'ts: If the event is a circumcision, be considerate of the parents and family. You know them better than I do, but it's a safe assumption that they will be quite nervous and apprehensive. Save your questions for other members of the family, the rabbi, or the *mohel,* and for after the circumcision itself. As in the case of the other home-based rituals, it is best not to bring food. You may, if you wish, bring a gift for the baby.

A final thought. *Don't* be intimidated or frightened by the *Brit Milah. Do* make every attempt to attend. It is the oldest Jewish ritual "in the book." It is moving and powerful and a moment that you'll not soon forget. Besides, in the years to come, you will always have the pleasure of reminding the young man, his wife, and his children that you were present at his *Bris*.

A *HANUKKAH* PARTY

You've read chapter 7 discussing the holiday of *Hanukkah* and you have some idea of the history and traditions surrounding the holiday. You understand that the holiday has increased in importance to American Jews because of its proximity to Christmas. And now you've been invited to a *Hanukkah* party. By this, I mean a Jewish *Hanukkah* party as distinguished from a combined Christmas–*Hanukkah* celebration at the office or country club (which is really likely to be a winter seasonal party without much religious content—I have no idea what to expect from such a combined affair). As you will see, there is no prescribed format for a *Hanukkah* party, much less an Americanized combination.

When: Because of the structure of the Jewish calendar, *Hanukkah* can take place anywhere from late November to late December. The most popular night for the *Hanukkah* party itself is the first night of the holiday, although you may find that the party takes place on any of the eight nights of *Hanukkah*. I hope that the party is truly a *Hanukkah* party and not a combined affair at which the family is celebrating both *Hanukkah* and Christmas. As you know, *Hanukkah* is a separate, significant Jewish holiday in its own right; it is not the "Jewish Christmas." The party is likely to be an evening affair since an important element is lighting the *Hanukkah* candles, which takes place just after sunset.

Who Will Be There: You can expect family, friends, relatives, and children from the neighborhood. You should not expect to find the rabbi, cantor, or any clergy. *Hanukkah* is a home-based celebration; the rabbi should be home with his or her family.

Where It Will Be Held: Most likely at your hosts' home.

What's Going to Happen: While a *Hanukkah* party can be as imaginative as your hosts, there are a few things that you can be sure will be present:

Image copyright of SweetChild Software

Figure 9: A *Hanukkah* Menorah

1. ***Hanukkah* Lights:** The heart of the *Hanukkah* celebration lies in lighting *Hanukkah* lights (usually candles but sometimes oil lamps or even electric lights). Each night we light the number of candles equal to the number of the night plus one *shamash* ("serving") candle used to light the others. Thus on the first night, we light the *shamash* plus one candle, on the second night, the *shamash* plus two candles, and so on until we light the full *menorah* on the eighth night (see figure 9). Before lighting the candles, two blessings are chanted, with an extra blessing recited on the first night. There may be one *menorah* for the whole family or party, or each family (or even each child) may be invited to bring their own.

2. ***Hanukkah* Foods:** Recalling that the miracle celebrated on *Hanukkah* deals with a small quantity of oil lasting far longer than expected, you should not be surprised to learn that foods containing oil are customarily eaten on *Hanukkah*. Ashkenazi

Figure 10: Several *Dreidels*

Jews prepare and devour greasy potato pancakes called *latkes* (this Yiddish word has no relation to the author's last name, but I did spend my childhood being called "potato head" by my Jewish friends). In Israel, deep-fried jelly rolls called *sufganiayot* are found during this time of year and no other. Other fried foods are also popular, so come prepared to forget your cholesterol level and diet.

3. ***Hanukkah* Games and Songs:** You will probably see the *Hanukkah* spinning top called a *dreidel* in Yiddish, or a *sivivon* in Hebrew (see figure 10). There are four Hebrew letters on the *dreidel* standing for the Hebrew phrase meaning "A Great Miracle Happened There." Children play a gambling game, often with chocolate coins called *Hanukkah Gelt,* which involves spinning the top and putting in and taking out coins depending on which letter is up when the *dreidel* stops

spinning. You will also be treated to a number of *Hanukkah* songs ranging from the traditional to the ridiculous.

4. ***Hanukkah* Gifts:** It is very likely that *Hanukkah* gifts will be exchanged at the party so it's best to check with your hosts to get some idea of what's expected of you. Each family will have its own approach, from small gifts for the children to a major gift exchange. You should have no trouble finding *Hanukkah* cards wherever greeting cards are sold in communities with a Jewish presence.

Do's and Don'ts: This is a light, fun-filled, "family and friends" celebration. Relax and enjoy yourself and don't be shy about asking questions. My only word of advice would be to treat *Hanukkah* as a Jewish holiday in its own right and not as "the Jewish Christmas." Yes, I know, you may well find that your host has a "*Hanukkah* Bush" and maybe even a Santa with a *kippah* appears (I really hope neither happens), but you can't go wrong playing it "straight." On the other hand, a cutesy *Hanukkah*/Christmas card (examples I've seen: Santa lighting *Hanukkah* candles, candy canes in the *menorah, Hanukkah* stockings with Jewish Stars on them, etc.) may not be in the best taste if your hosts are trying to create a separate *Hanukkah* identity and spirit. My advice would be to bring *Hanukkah* (and not Christmas) gifts for your Jewish friends and family members.

The greeting of the evening: "Happy *Hanukkah*!" or *"Chag Samayach!"*

A JEWISH WEDDING

Being married and having children are considered important *mitzvot* (commandments) in Judaism. Indeed, the first commandment God gives to humankind is to "be fertile and increase" (Gen 1:28). Jewish clergy are allowed, indeed encouraged, to marry.[92] The sacred nature of marriage is reflected in one of the Hebrew names given to the ceremony, *Kiddushin* (literally "holiness").

---

92. A true story: In the course of teaching about Judaism at area Catholic schools, I was reviewing questions submitted in writing in advance of the lesson by seventh grade students. My all-time favorite was "Do rabbis need to remain *obstinate*?" Rabbis are in fact strongly discouraged from being both obstinate and abstinent.

When: A Jewish marriage may take place any day of the week except for the Sabbath. Saturday evenings (after sundown) or Sundays are quite popular in the United States. While weddings are prohibited on certain Jewish holidays and portions of the Jewish calendar, this is your hosts' planning problem and not yours.

Who Will Be There: Anyone and everyone you'd expect. Presiding will be a rabbi or cantor or both.

Where It Will Be Held: Traditionally, many weddings took place in the groom's home, in order to include the site of the new Jewish home in the ceremony itself. The wedding canopy (Hebrew *chuppah*) that the bride and groom stand under (it may be a floral construction, or a *tallit,* or some other beautiful creation) symbolizes this home. Today, the site of the wedding may be a synagogue, a catering hall, someone's home, or even out in nature (where the canopy is augmented by God's own canopy of the sky and stars).

What's Going to Happen: There is wide variation in wedding customs in different communities, movements, and cultures. The following will give you the highlights that you are most likely to see. Do enjoy and ask about the variations that you find.

Male guests will probably be provided with head coverings as they enter the ceremony room or area. The processional of families may range from the traditional, where the groom and his parents and the men enter first and the bride, her parents, and her escorts circle the groom seven times (corresponding to the seven verses in the Bible that contain the phrase "and when a man takes a wife" [93]), to a more Western procession of key family members and honorees. Once everyone is under the *chuppah,* the rabbi will pronounce a series of blessings, and the bride and groom will drink from the same cup of wine. The groom places a ring (traditionally solid metal so its value is unambiguous) on the right forefinger of the bride's hand (some believe this finger has a direct link to the heart), and recites the traditional formula *"Ha-rei aht me-ku-deshet li be-ta-ba'aht zoh, ke daht Moshe ve-Yisrael"* ("You are hereby sanctified unto me with this ring according to the laws of Moses and Israel"). In many non-Orthodox

---

93. Isaac Klein, *A Guide to Jewish Religious Practice,* The Jewish Theological Seminary of America, 1979, p. 401.

ceremonies, the bride may also place a ring on the groom's finger and recite a similar formula. The rabbi may then read or summarize the marriage contract (Hebrew *ketubbah*), and then recite or chant the traditional seven wedding blessings.

The conclusion of the ceremony is punctuated by the groom smashing a glass underfoot. This tradition is generally understood to be symbolic of the fact that since the Temple and Jerusalem have not been rebuilt, we need to temper our joy even at the happiest moments. Others believe that the breaking of the glass is a vestige of an action designed to frighten away evil spirits. Whatever the origin, the response from the crowd is *mazel tov* (congratulations and good luck) as bride and groom kiss and exit. In traditional ceremonies, the bride and groom will spend the next few minutes alone together, symbolizing their private married life. For very traditional Jews, this may be their first unchaperoned moments together.

Do's and Don'ts: Do enjoy yourself and don't worry. At very traditional Orthodox weddings, you may find that men and women do not dance with one another. Use your good judgment and take cues from your hosts. It is entirely appropriate to bring wedding gifts to the ceremony and reception.

JEWISH FUNERALS AND CONDOLENCE CALLS

All of the events discussed above are happy events, celebrations. While no one would call a funeral a happy event, you may well sense a feeling of celebrating a life well lived at a Jewish funeral. The Jewish attitude toward death is one that confronts the reality of death and the need to mourn. Judaism does not embrace the "stiff upper lip" approach and does not encourage mourners to get back into the swing of life as soon as possible. On the contrary, Judaism emphasizes the need to mourn and acknowledge the life that has been lived and that is now missed. There are three distinct periods to the mourning:

1. **From the moment of death until the funeral:** During this period, the focus is on the deceased and the funeral. Jewish law exempts close family members from many positive commandments such as daily prayer. They will be attending to the

funeral arrangements during this period. Tradition suggests
that you not visit the family during this period.

2. **The funeral and the week following the funeral:** During
this period, the focus is on the mourners. The Bible (Job 2:13)
tells us that Job's friends sat silently with him for a period of
seven days as he mourned the loss of his children. This period
is generally called "sitting *shivah*" (*shivah* is the Hebrew
word for seven); it is a time for you and others to visit the
family and extend condolences.

3. **The period past *shivah:*** Jewish law provides an extended
thirty-day period of mourning for the death of siblings, children, and spouses and a period of one year for parents, during
which restrictive guidelines, such as the prohibition against
attending public festivities, might be observed.

The most common time for you to be invited to comfort mourners is
at the funeral itself and at the *shivah* home.

When: Jewish law provides that a funeral will take place
within a day of death but never just before (i.e., Friday afternoon) or
on *Shabbat* or a holy day itself. In practice, the funeral may be
delayed a day or two to allow relatives and friends from out of town
to attend. Judaism does not have a wake per se. The *shivah* period of
seven days of mourning (the Sabbath counts as a day but formal
mourning does not take place on this day and visiting the mourners
is not customarily encouraged) immediately follows the funeral.
You may hear the family discuss a daily *minyan* to take place at the
home. A *minyan,* or quorum of ten Jews (traditionally ten men), is
required in order to recite certain prayers including the Mourners'
Kaddish; the term is often used for the prayer service itself as in "the
minyan this evening is at 7:00 P.M." It is customary for friends and
family of the mourners to arrange for such daily prayers to take
place at the home during *shivah*. Although non-Jews are not physi-
cally counted in the *minyan,* you would probably be welcome to
attend. The service itself is a daily prayer service (see above), probably led by a friend or relative (a rabbi may be present but is not
necessary), often with the inclusion of some special readings for a
house of mourning. There may be study sessions of traditional
sacred literature as well.

Who Will Be There: In addition to the expected mix of friends, family, and business associates at the funeral home and *shivah* home, you should expect a rabbi or cantor, or both, presiding at the funeral.

Where It Will Be Held: The funeral will generally be at a funeral home and rarely at a synagogue. The funeral home may or may not be located at the cemetery. Occasionally, if the funeral has already taken place (for example, in another town), or if there has been a cremation (although Jewish law forbids cremation, it is not uncommon among less observant Jews), you may find that a memorial service has been planned. This service may well be at a synagogue or someone's home.

What's Going to Happen:
1. **Funeral:** As you arrive at the funeral home, men will be given head coverings and there will be an initial period when the attendees greet one another. The immediate family of the deceased may or may not be present with you during this period. They may be spending a few final moments with the deceased and the rabbi, who will be assisting them in the ritual of the tearing of their garments or of a symbolic ribbon. The service will be called to order in a room with the casket present and closed (Jewish law does not favor viewings, as they are considered disrespectful of the dead). The family may be in the front rows, secluded off to one side, or behind a curtain. The rabbi or cantor will lead the congregation in prayers (in both English and Hebrew); you will often be given a pamphlet with some of the prayers so you can follow along. In addition to the prayers, there will be a eulogy delivered by the rabbi, by a family member or members, and/or by one or more friends. Frequently, a few words will be said by several people. The goal is to assist the mourners in releasing the emotion of the moment and to begin the bereavement process, as well as to bring dignity to the memory of the departed. Crying is perfectly okay; in fact, in some Jewish cultures, professional mourners were hired to help achieve this same end. After the service in the funeral home, there will be a graveside service with recitation of the Mourners' *Kaddish* and burial. It is considered a *mitzvah* for members of the family and friends

to assist with the interment by tossing a bit of earth into the grave. You will be given instructions.

2. ***Shivah* Home:** Immediately after the funeral, the family and guests assemble at the designated place for a traditional "meal of condolence." This generally takes place whether or not the family is "sitting *shivah*." You will be given directions and often a map to the location. At the home, it is customary to have a pitcher of water just outside the home in order to purify yourself ritually (having come in contact with death at the cemetery) by pouring water over your hands as biblically prescribed. An elaborate table of foods will usually await the family and guests, often including hard-boiled eggs as a symbol of the renewal of life. Tradition provides that the mourners need not worry about preparing meals during the *shivah* period. The mood may range from mournful to cheerful as the life of the deceased is recalled, depending on the circumstances of the loved one's death. You may find that the mirrors in the home have been turned toward the wall or covered. This is a tradition that is in the spirit of not caring about one's appearance. Jewish law provides that mourners not adorn themselves (traditionally, men don't shave, women don't wear cosmetics, leather shoes are not worn) and that they sit on low chairs. These laws may or may not be observed in the home you are visiting. A memorial candle will burn during the seven-day period.

Do's and Don'ts: The first and most important rule is **do call and do go!** This applies to both the funeral and *shivah* visits. Although you may think the family wants to be alone and not talk to you in their grief, you should still call. If they are not observing *shivah,* they will let you know when and if to come; if they are sitting *shivah,* this means visitors are expected (indeed, commanded—it's a *mitzvah* or commandment to visit) and welcome. You should call if you are coming at an odd time. If you can, try to visit during times when other visitors might not attend, such as after the initial day or on weekdays. Plan to stay for about thirty minutes, The tradition of sending flowers, which stems from the need to provide perfume for the decaying body, has been frowned upon by Judaism, which provides for prompt interment. If you wish to pay respects in a material way, you might make a contribution in memory of the deceased to a charity that will be announced by the family, or to a charity of your own choice in the name of the deceased. Regarding other aspects of the funeral, use your common sense as you would with any funeral. Children are welcome so long as they are mature enough to be well-behaved.

When you pay a *shivah* visit, Jewish tradition provides the following etiquette. Enter the room quietly and sit down next to the mourner(s). Say little or nothing. Be guided by the mourners as to whether to talk and what to talk about. It's not what you say but your presence that counts. Having lost both my parents, I know firsthand how comforting it is to be in the presence and embrace of friends and family, even those—maybe especially those—whom I haven't seen for years and who may feel most awkward about coming. Once again, it's fine to bring children unless you are asked not to. Children remind us all of the continuity of life and the promise of the future.

BOTTOM LINES ABOUT ATTENDING JEWISH EVENTS

The most important advice that I can give you about attending a Jewish event is **relax and enjoy.** Your hosts know that you are not Jewish and understand that you will not be familiar with every detail. Absorb the environment and the experience, including the sights, smells, and sounds. Reflect, if you are so inclined, that if Jesus were present, he would have no problem following the Hebrew and the flow of the event. Indeed, he certainly did attend similar events during his lifetime.

Drink in the joy of being a part of another way of praising God. Try to see some of the origins of your own Christian practices in the ceremonies that you've witnessed. Some of these common elements, such as the ceremonial bread and wine, will be easy to spot. Others will be more subtle; look at the *tallit* or prayer shawl that the clergy and many of the congregants wear during services. In what ways does it resemble the vestments of the clergy at your own church? If you have an English translation of the prayers available, do you recognize any prayers from your own liturgy? A common blessing at Jewish services is the Priestly Blessing: "May the LORD bless you and keep you. May the LORD deal kindly with you and graciously with you. May the LORD bestow His favor upon you and grant you peace" (Num 6:24–26).

I wish you a meaningful and spiritually fulfilling experience at these events.

Appendix 1
Dabru Emet: A Jewish Statement on Christians and Christianity

In recent years, there has been a dramatic and unprecedented shift in Jewish and Christian relations. Throughout the nearly two millennia of Jewish exile, Christians have tended to characterize Judaism as a failed religion or, at best, a religion that prepared the way for, and is completed in, Christianity. In the decades since the Holocaust, however, Christianity has changed dramatically. An increasing number of official Church bodies, both Roman Catholic and Protestant, have made public statements of their remorse about Christian mistreatment of Jews and Judaism. These statements have declared, furthermore, that Christian teaching and preaching can and must be reformed so that they acknowledge God's enduring covenant with the Jewish people and celebrate the contribution of Judaism to world civilization and to Christian faith itself.

We believe these changes merit a thoughtful Jewish response. Speaking only for ourselves—an interdenominational group of Jewish scholars—we believe it is time for Jews to learn about the efforts of Christians to honor Judaism. We believe it is time for Jews to reflect on what Judaism may now say about Christianity. As a first step, we offer eight brief statements about how Jews and Christians may relate to one another.

Jews and Christians worship the same God. Before the rise of Christianity, Jews were the only worshippers of the God of Israel. But Christians also worship the God of Abraham, Isaac, and Jacob; creator of heaven and earth. While Christian worship is not a viable religious choice for Jews, as Jewish theologians we rejoice that, through

Christianity, hundreds of millions of people have entered into relationship with the God of Israel.

Jews and Christians seek authority from the same book — the Bible (what Jews call "Tanakh" and Christians call the "Old Testament"). Turning to it for religious orientation, spiritual enrichment, and communal education, we each take away similar lessons: God created and sustains the universe; God established a covenant with the people Israel; God's revealed word guides Israel to a life of righteousness; and God will ultimately redeem Israel and the whole world. Yet, Jews and Christians interpret the Bible differently on many points. Such differences must always be respected.

Christians can respect the claim of the Jewish people upon the land of Israel. The most important event for Jews since the Holocaust has been the reestablishment of a Jewish state in the Promised Land. As members of a biblically based religion, Christians appreciate that Israel was promised — and given — to Jews as the physical center of the covenant between them and God. Many Christians support the State of Israel for reasons far more profound than mere politics. As Jews, we applaud this support. We also recognize that Jewish tradition mandates justice for all non-Jews who reside in a Jewish state.

Jews and Christians accept the moral principles of Torah. Central to the moral principles of Torah is the inalienable sanctity and dignity of every human being. All of us were created in the image of God. This shared moral emphasis can be the basis of an improved relationship between our two communities. It can also be the basis of a powerful witness to all humanity for improving the lives of our fellow human beings and for standing against the immoralities and idolatries that harm and degrade us. Such witness is especially needed after the unprecedented horrors of the past century.

Nazism was not a Christian phenomenon. Without the long history of Christian anti-Judaism and Christian violence against Jews, Nazi ideology could not have taken hold nor could it have been carried out. Too many Christians participated in, or were sympathetic to, Nazi atrocities against Jews. Other Christians did not protest sufficiently against these atrocities. But Nazism itself was not an inevitable outcome of Christianity. If the Nazi extermination of the Jews had been fully successful, it would have turned its murderous rage more directly to Christians. We recognize with gratitude those Christians who risked or sacrificed their lives to save Jews during the Nazi regime. With that in mind, we encourage the continuation of recent efforts in Christian theology to repudiate unequivocally contempt of Judaism and the Jewish people. We applaud those Christians who reject this teaching of contempt, and we do not blame them for the sins committed by their ancestors.

The humanly irreconcilable difference between Jews and Christians will not be settled until God redeems the entire world as promised in Scripture. Christians know and serve God through Jesus Christ and the Christian tradition. Jews know and serve God through Torah and the Jewish tradition. That difference will not be settled by one community insisting that it has interpreted Scripture more accurately than the other; nor by exercising political power over the other. Jews can respect Christians' faithfulness to their revelation just as we expect Christians to respect our faithfulness to our revelation. Neither Jew nor Christian should be pressed into affirming the teaching of the other community.

A new relationship between Jews and Christians will not weaken Jewish practice. An improved relationship will not accelerate the cultural and religious assimilation that Jews rightly fear. It will not change traditional Jewish forms of worship, nor increase intermarriage between Jews and non-Jews, nor persuade more Jews to convert to Christianity, nor create a false blending of Judaism and Christianity. We respect Christianity as a faith that originated within Judaism and that still has significant contacts with it. We do not see it as an extension of Judaism. Only if we cherish our own traditions can we pursue this relationship with integrity.

Jews and Christians must work together for justice and peace. Jews and Christians, each in their own way, recognize the unredeemed state of the world as reflected in the persistence of persecution, poverty, and human degradation and misery. Although justice and peace are finally God's, our joint efforts, together with those of other faith communities, will help bring the kingdom of God for which we hope and long. Separately and together, we must work to bring justice and peace to our world. In this enterprise, we are guided by the vision of the prophets of Israel:

> It shall come to pass in the end of days that the mountain of
> the LORD's house shall be established at the top of the

mountains and be exalted above the hills, and the nations shall flow unto it...and many peoples shall go and say, "Come ye and let us go up to the mountain of the LORD to the house of the God of Jacob and He will teach us of His ways and we will walk in his paths." (Isa 2:2–3)

Tikva Frymer-Kensky, University of Chicago
David Novak, University of Toronto
Peter Ochs, University of Virginia
Michael Signer, University of Notre Dame

[NOTE: As of July 29, 2002, this statement had been signed by 222 Jewish scholars and clergy.]

Appendix 2
A Sacred Obligation:
Rethinking Christian Faith in Relation to Judaism and the Jewish People:
A Statement by the Christian Scholars Group on Christian-Jewish Relations

September 1, 2002

Since its inception in 1969, the Christian Scholars Group has been seeking to develop more adequate Christian theologies of the church's relationship to Judaism and the Jewish people. Pursuing this work for over three decades under varied sponsorship, members of our association of Protestant and Roman Catholic biblical scholars, historians, and theologians have published many volumes on Christian-Jewish relations.

Our work has a historical context. For most of the past two thousand years, Christians have erroneously portrayed Jews as unfaithful, holding them collectively responsible for the death of Jesus and therefore accursed by God. In agreement with many official Christian declarations, we reject this accusation as historically false and theologically invalid. It suggests that God can be unfaithful to the eternal covenant with the Jewish people. We acknowledge with shame the suffering this distorted portrayal has brought upon the Jewish people. We repent of this teaching of contempt. Our repentance requires us to build a new teaching of respect. This task is important at any time, but the deadly crisis in the Middle East and the frightening resurgence of antisemitism worldwide give it particular urgency.

We believe that revising Christian teaching about Judaism and the Jewish people is a central and indispensable obligation of theology in our time. It is essential that Christianity both understand and represent Judaism accurately, not only as a matter of justice for the Jewish people, but also for the integrity of Christian faith, which we cannot proclaim without reference to Judaism. Moreover, since there is a unique bond between Christianity and Judaism, revitalizing our appreciation of Jewish religious life will deepen our Christian faith. We base these convictions on ongoing scholarly research and the official statements of many Christian denominations over the past fifty years.

We are grateful for the willingness of many Jews to engage in dialogue and study with us. We welcomed it when, on September 10, 2000, Jewish scholars sponsored by the Institute of Christian and Jewish Studies in Baltimore issued a historic declaration, *Dabru Emet: A Jewish Statement on Christians and Christianity*. This document, affirmed by notable rabbis and Jewish scholars, called on Jews to re-examine their understanding of Christianity.

Encouraged by the work of both Jewish and Christian colleagues, we offer the following ten statements for the consideration of our fellow Christians. We urge all Christians to reflect on their faith in light of these statements. For us, this is a sacred obligation.

1. God's covenant with the Jewish people endures forever. For centuries Christians claimed that their covenant with God replaced or superseded the Jewish covenant. We renounce this claim. We believe that God does not revoke divine promises. We affirm that God is in covenant with both Jews and Christians. Tragically, the entrenched theology of supersessionism continues to influence Christian faith, worship, and practice, even though it has been repudiated by many Christian denominations and many Christians no longer accept it. Our recognition of the abiding validity of Judaism has implications for all aspects of Christian life.

2. Jesus of Nazareth lived and died as a faithful Jew. Christians worship the God of Israel in and through Jesus Christ. Supersessionism, however, prompted Christians over the centuries to speak of Jesus as an opponent of Judaism. This is historically incorrect. Jewish worship, ethics, and practice shaped Jesus' life and teachings. The scriptures of his people inspired and nurtured him. Christian preaching and teaching today must describe Jesus' earthly life as engaged in the ongoing Jewish quest to live out God's covenant in everyday life.

3. Ancient rivalries must not define Christian-Jewish relations today. Although today we know Christianity and Judaism as separate religions, what became the church was a movement within the Jewish community for many decades after the ministry and resurrection of Jesus. The destruction of the Jerusalem Temple by Roman armies in the year 70 of the first century caused a crisis among the Jewish people. Various groups, including Christianity and early rabbinic Judaism, competed for leadership in the Jewish community by claiming that they were the true heirs of biblical Israel. The gospels reflect this rivalry in which the disputants exchanged various accusations. Christian charges of hypocrisy and legalism misrepresent Judaism and constitute an unworthy foundation for Christian self-understanding.

4. Judaism is a living faith, enriched by many centuries of development. Many Christians mistakenly equate Judaism with biblical Israel. However, Judaism, like Christianity, developed new modes of belief and practice in the centuries after the destruction of the Temple. The rabbinic tradition gave new emphasis and understanding to existing practices, such as communal prayer, study of Torah, and deeds of loving-kindness. Thus Jews could live out the covenant in a world without the Temple. Over time they developed an extensive body of interpretive literature that continues to enrich Jewish life, faith, and self-understanding. Christians cannot fully understand Judaism apart from its post-biblical development, which can also enrich and enhance Christian faith.

5. The Bible both connects and separates Jews and Christians. Some Jews and Christians today, in the process of studying the Bible together, are discovering new ways of reading that provide a deeper appreciation of both traditions. While the two communities draw from the same biblical texts of ancient Israel, they have developed different traditions of interpretation. Christians view these texts through the lens of the New Testament, while Jews understand these scriptures through the traditions of rabbinic commentary.

Referring to the first part of the Christian Bible as the "Old Testament" can wrongly suggest that these texts are obsolete.

Alternative expressions—"Hebrew Bible," "First Testament," or "Shared Testament"—although also problematic, may better express the church's renewed appreciation of the ongoing power of these scriptures for both Jews and Christians.

6. Affirming God's enduring covenant with the Jewish people has consequences for Christian understandings of salvation. Christians meet God's saving power in the person of Jesus Christ and believe that this power is available to all people in him. Christians have therefore taught for centuries that salvation is available only through Jesus Christ. With their recent realization that God's covenant with the Jewish people is eternal, Christians can now recognize in the Jewish tradition the redemptive power of God at work. If Jews, who do not share our faith in Christ, are in a saving covenant with God, then Christians need new ways of understanding the universal significance of Christ.

7. Christians should not target Jews for conversion. In view of our conviction that Jews are in an eternal covenant with God, we renounce missionary efforts directed at converting Jews. At the same time, we welcome opportunities for Jews and Christians to bear witness to their respective experiences of God's saving ways. Neither can properly claim to possess knowledge of God entirely or exclusively.

8. Christian worship that teaches contempt for Judaism dishonors God. The New Testament contains passages that have frequently generated negative attitudes toward Jews and Judaism. The use of these texts in the context of worship increases the likelihood of hostility toward Jews. Christian anti-Jewish theology has also shaped worship in ways that denigrate Judaism and foster contempt for Jews. We urge church leaders to examine scripture readings, prayers, the structure of the lectionaries, preaching, and hymns to remove distorted images of Judaism. A reformed Christian liturgical life would express a new relationship with Jews and thus honor God.

9. We affirm the importance of the land of Israel for the life of the Jewish people. The land of Israel has always been of central significance to the Jewish people. However, Christian theology charged that the Jews had condemned themselves to homelessness by rejecting God's Messiah. Such supersessionism precluded any possibility for

Christian understanding of Jewish attachment to the land of Israel. Christian theologians can no longer avoid this crucial issue, especially in light of the complex and persistent conflict over the land. Recognizing that both Israelis and Palestinians have the right to live in peace and security in a homeland of their own, we call for efforts that contribute to a just peace among all the peoples in the region.

10. Christians should work with Jews for the healing of the world. For almost a century, Jews and Christians in the United States have worked together on important social issues, such as the rights of workers and civil rights. As violence and terrorism intensify in our time, we must strengthen our common efforts in the work of justice and peace to which both the prophets of Israel and Jesus summon us. These common efforts by Jews and Christians offer a vision of human solidarity and provide models of collaboration with people of other faith traditions.

Signed by members of the
Christian Scholars Group on Christian-Jewish Relations

Institutions listed only for identification purposes.

Dr. Norman Beck, Poehlmann Professor of Biblical Theology and Classical Languages, Texas Lutheran University Seguin, Texas

Dr. Mary C. Boys, SNJM, Skinner & McAlpin Professor of Practical Theology, Union Theological Seminary, New York City, New York

Dr. Rosann Catalano, Roman Catholic Staff Scholar, Institute for Christian & Jewish Studies, Baltimore, Maryland

Dr. Philip A. Cunningham, Executive Director Center for Christian-Jewish Learning, Boston College, Chestnut Hill, Massachusetts

Dr. Celia Deutsch, NDS, Adjunct Associate Professor of Religion, Barnard College/Columbia University, New York City, New York

Dr. Alice L. Eckardt, Professor Emerita of Religion Studies, Lehigh University, Bethlehem, Pennsylvania

Dr. Eugene J. Fisher, U.S. Conference of Catholic Bishops' Committee for Ecumenical and Interreligious Affairs, Washington, D.C.

Dr. Eva Fleischner, Montclair (NJ) State University, Emerita, Claremont, California

Dr. Deirdre Good, General Theological Seminary of the Episcopal Church, New York City, New York

Dr. Walter Harrelson, Distinguished Professor Emeritus of Hebrew Bible, Vanderbilt University, Nashville, Tennessee

Rev. Michael McGarry, CSP, Tantur Ecumenical Institute, Jerusalem

Dr. John C. Merkle, Professor of Theology, College of St. Benedict, St. Joseph, Minnesota

Dr. John T. Pawlikowski, OSM, Professor of Social Ethics, Director, Catholic-Jewish Studies Program, Catholic Theological Union, Chicago, Illinois

Dr. Peter A. Pettit, Institute for Christian-Jewish Understanding, Muhlenberg College, Allentown, Pennsylvania

Dr. Peter C. Phan, The Warren-Blanding Professor of Religion and Culture, The Catholic University of America, Washington, D.C.

Dr. Jean Pierre Ruiz, Associate Professor and Chair, Department of Theology and Religious Studies, St. John's University, New York City, New York

Dr. Franklin Sherman, Associate for Interfaith Relations, Evangelical Lutheran Church in America, Allentown, Pennsylvania

Dr. Joann Spillman, Professor and Chair, Department of Theology and Religious Studies, Rockhurst University, Kansas City, Missouri

Dr. John T. Townsend, Visiting Lecturer on Jewish Studies, Harvard Divinity School, Cambridge, Massachusetts

Dr. Joseph Tyson, Professor Emeritus of Religious Studies, Southern Methodist University, Dallas, Texas

Dr. Clark M. Williamson, Indiana Professor of Christian Thought, Emeritus, Christian Theological Seminary, Indianapolis, Indiana

Glossary

In the following list, I have tried to include most of the terms that you might come across as you read this book and others on Judaism as well as around the dining room table in a Jewish home. Words printed in bold within the definitions are entries themselve. For many more terms as well as more complete definitions, I recommend the *JPS Dictionary of Jewish Words* by Joyce Eisenberg and Ellen Scolnic (Jewish Publication Society, 2001). With permission of the Jewish Publication Society, I have adopted their pronunciation guide presented in parentheses after each word.

Adonai (ah-doe-NYE): Hebrew word used when God's four-letter name is read in the Torah or in a prayer. Literally "My Lord."

afikoman (ah-fee-KO-men): The piece of **matzah** that is hidden in a Passover **Seder** for the children to find at the end of the meal.

aggadah (ah-gah-DAH): Jewish stories and folktales presented in the **Talmud.**

Aleinu (ah-LAY-noo): One of the concluding prayers of the Jewish service. Worshipers traditionally stand and bow during this prayer.

aliyah (ah-LEE-yah), pl. **aliyot** (ah-LEE-yot): The honor of being called up to say a blessing or read from the Torah scroll (or participate in some other honor) at a synagogue service.

amen (ah-MEN): Said at the conclusion of many prayers by the congregation to indicate their agreement with the prayer. A Hebrew word, it literally means "so be it."

Amidah (ah-MEE-dah): Central prayer of each synagogue service, literally meaning "standing." The prayer is actually said standing. Often this prayer is called by other names—**Tefilah** or the names of its first two sections, *Avot* (ah-VOTE) and *Givurot* (giv-ur-OTE).

Aramaic (ar-ah-MAY-ick): Ancient Semitic language spoken in late biblical times, it is the language of the **Talmud,** the **ketubbah,** and several of the most important prayers.

aron kodesh (ah-ROAN CO-desh): The ark, or cabinet, at the front of the synagogue that holds the scrolls of the **Torah.**

Ashkenazim (osh-ken-NAH-zeem): Hebrew name given to that group of Jews who trace their ancestry to Germany and Eastern Europe. Most American Jews belong to this group.

Bar/Bat Mitzvah (BAR/BAT MITS-vah): The "coming of age" ritual for boys (at age thirteen) and girls (at age twelve, traditionally, thirteen in many congregations), usually marked by the child leading a Sabbath service and reading from the **Torah.** Literally "Son/Daughter of Commandment."

Barchu (bar-KHOO): The call to worship that begins the principal part of each morning and evening synagogue service.

B.C.E.: Abbreviation for "Before the Common Era," used by Jews instead of B.C. ("Before Christ').

beit knesset (BAYT kuh-NESS-et): Literally "House of Gathering," this is the Hebrew word for **synagogue.**

bimah (BEE-mah): Raised area at the front or center of a synagogue from which the **Torah** is read.

Birkat Hamazon (beer-KHAT hah-mah-ZONE): Traditional blessing said after eating a meal.

B'nai Mitzvah (buh-NAY MITS-vah): Plural for **Bar** or **Bar** and **Bat Mitzvah.** Literally "Children of Commandment."

bracha (brah-KHAH), pl. **brachot** (brah-KHOTE): A type of prayer (literally "blessing") that begins with the formula *Baruch ata Adonai*

(Blessed are You, Adonai), said before eating and before performing many **mitzvot.**

Bris (BRISS): Yiddish for circumcision ceremony.

Brit Milah (BREET mee-LAH): Hebrew for circumcision ceremony, literally "covenant of circumcision."

brucha (BRAW-khuh): Yiddish pronunciation of **bracha.**

cantor: English term for clergy person who leads congregation in prayer and singing; called **chazzan** in Hebrew.

C.E.: Abbreviation for Common Era, used by Jews instead of A.D. (*anno Domini,* meaning "year of our Lord").

Chabad Lubavitch Movement (khah-BAHD luh-BOVE-itch): One of the best known **Chasidic** sects.

chai (KHIGH): Hebrew for life, this word is often found as a decorative charm worn around the neck. Since the two Hebrew letters that make up this word have a numerical value of 18, Jews often give charitable contributions and gifts as multiples of 18.

challah (hah-LAH): Braided egg bread traditionally eaten on the Sabbath.

chametz (hah-MAYTS): Literally "leaven," this term is used to describe foods prohibited on Passover.

Chanukah see **Hanukkah**

Chasidism (or **Hasidism**) (HAH-see-dizm): A movement of ultra-orthodox Jews founded in the eighteenth century in Poland.

chazzan (or **hazzan**) (HAH-zin): Hebrew term for cantor.

Chumash (or **Humash**) (hoo-MASH): Hebrew term for a book containing the Torah or the Five Books of Moses.

chuppah (or **huppah**) (HUH-pah): Jewish wedding canopy.

cohen (or **kohen**) (CO-hane), pl. **cohanim:** Hebrew for priest; this is a man who traces his ancestry to Aaron (the brother of Moses) and who, as a result, is subject to certain privileges and responsibilities under Jewish law.

daven (DAH-ven): Yiddish for pray.

diaspora: English term (from the Greek meaning "dispersion") for Jews and their communities outside the land of Israel.

dreidel (DRAY-duhl): Yiddish for a small, four-sided spinning top used on **Hanukkah.**

Elohim (eh-loe-HEEM): One of many Hebrew words used to designate "God."

Eretz Yisra'el (EH-rets yis-rah-ALE): Hebrew for the land of Israel.

erev (EH-rev): Literally "evening," this Hebrew term is used for the evening before the Sabbath (as in **Erev Shabbat**) and holidays since the Jewish day begins at sunset.

fleishig (FLAY-shick): Yiddish word for foods in the meat category and therefore not mixable with milk products under the **kosher** laws.

Four Questions: Special ritual questions asked during the **Passover Seder,** usually by the youngest present.

frum (FROM): A Yiddish word meaning religious.

Gan Eden (GAHN AYE-den): Hebrew for the Garden of Eden.

G-d: The respectful way traditional Jews write the word "God" so as to avoid a written name on paper that might be destroyed or erased.

gefilte fish (guh-FILL-teh FISH): A ground patty of fish, eggs, and matzah meal that is traditionally served at festive meals.

gelt (GELT): Yiddish for money. Chocolate foil-wrapped coins given at **Hanukkah** are commonly seen and are called **Hanukkah Gelt.**

Gemara (guh-MAR-ah): The **Aramaic** word for learning, it is the commentary on the **Mishna;** the **Mishna,** together with the **Gemara,** comprise the **Talmud.**

get (GEHT): Hebrew term for divorce decree.

gevalt (guh-VOLT): Yiddish expression of surprise, commonly heard as **Oy Gevalt.**

ghetto: Restricted area in European cities in which Jews were required to live.

glatt kosher (GLOT CO-sher): Yiddish for strictly kosher.

goy (GOY), pl. **goyim** (GOY-eem): Hebrew word that literally means "nation," it has come to be a pejorative term for a non-Jew.

grager (GROG-er): Yiddish word for the rattle or noisemaker used during **Purim** services and celebrations.

gut Shabbos (GUHT SHA-bos): Yiddish term of greeting on the Sabbath, literally "Good Sabbath."

Hadassah (hah-DAS-sah): Jewish women's charitable organization.

haftarah (hoff-TOE-rah): Hebrew word meaning "conclusion," this refers to the portion of the prophetic books of the Bible chanted in **synagogue** during **Shabbat** morning services.

Haggadah (hah-GAH-dah): The collection of prayers, stories, and songs used for the home celebration of the **Passover Seder.** Hebrew for "telling."

hag sameach (HAG sah-MAY-ach): Hebrew greeting meaning "Happy Holiday."

hakafah (hah-kah-FAH): Hebrew term for the procession of carrying the **Torah** throughout the congregation prior to its reading.

halacha (hah-lah-KHAH): Hebrew term for Jewish law.

Haman (HEY-man): The villain of the **Purim** story as told in the biblical book of Esther.

hamantashen (HUM-min-TOSH-in): Yiddish name for the triangular pastries traditionally eaten on Purim, it is Yiddish for Haman's ears.

hametz (hah-MAYTS): Hebrew for leaven, this class of foods is prohibited on Passover.

ha-Motzi (hah-MOE-tsee): Familiar blessing said before eating bread.

hamsa (HAHM-sah): An amulet charm worn around the neck or hung on a wall. The term comes from the Arabic word for "five"—an allusion to the five fingers of the hand of God—because the amulet is shaped like a hand, symbolizing the protective hand of God.

Hanukkah (or **Chanukah**) (HAH-noo-kah): Wintertime celebration of the holiday of lights, it is a Hebrew word that means "dedication," referring to the rededication of the Temple after the successful Maccabee revolt.

haroset (hah-ROE-set): Hebrew for the mixture of chopped nuts, apples, and wine served at Passover **Seders.** This treat symbolizes the mortar that was used by enslaved Hebrews to make bricks in Egypt.

ha-Shem (hah-SHEM): Hebrew meaning "the name," this term is used by traditional Jews to avoid using an English or Hebrew word for God in common conversation.

Hatikvah (hah-TICK-vah): The national anthem of the State of Israel. Hebrew meaning "the hope."

Havah Nagilah (HAH-vah nug-GEEL-ah): Traditional Jewish song played at weddings, **Bar/Bat Mitzvah,** and so forth.

Havdalah (hav-DOLL-ah): Hebrew for separation, this is the ceremony signaling the end of the Sabbath at sundown on Saturday.

High Holidays or High Holy Days: The ten-day period including the two Jewish holidays of **Rosh Hashanah** and **Yom Kippur.**

hora (HOE-rah): Traditional circular folkdance.

Jew by Choice: Common term for a convert to Judaism.

Jew for Jesus or Messianic Jew: Member of a religious movement who believes that he or she is Jewish but holds that Jesus is the Jewish Messiah and God. Jews for Jesus are considered by both Judaism and Christianity to be Christians.

kabbalah (kah-buh-LAH): Hebrew word literally meaning "received (tradition)," this is the term for Jewish mysticism. From the Hebrew word for "holy."

Kaddish (KAH-dish): The prayer recited several times during a Jewish service but especially noted for its recitation to honor someone who has died. From the Hebrew word for "holy."

karpas (CAR-pas): Hebrew term for the green vegetable eaten during the Passover **Seder,** symbolizing spring.

kashrut (KOSH-root): The Jewish dietary laws that specify what is **kosher.**

ketubbah (keh-TOO-bah): The Jewish marriage contract.

kibbutz (kih-BOOTS): Hebrew term for a collective farm.

kibitz (KIB-its): Yiddish term for joking around, giving (often unwelcome) advice, wisecracking, and so forth.

kiddush (KID-ish): Hebrew for blessing said over wine in honor of the Sabbath or a holy day.

kiddushin (kee-doo-SHEEN): Literally "sanctification" or "holiness," this is one of the names for the Jewish wedding ceremony.

kippah (KEE-pah); pl. **kippot** (kee-POTE): Hebrew for the skullcap worn by observant Jewish men.

klutz (KLUTZ): Yiddish for awkward or clumsy person.

Kol Nidre (coal KNEE-dray): The prayer that opens the **Yom Kippur** eve service.

kosher (CO-sher): Food that is acceptable according to Jewish dietary laws. The Hebrew word **kosher** means "fit" and is also applied to other items such as **Torah** scrolls, **mezuzot,** and so forth

kosher for Passover (or **Pesach**): Food that has been certified as meeting the more stringent standards that apply during this holiday.

kvell (KVELL): Yiddish term describing the special pride that parents feel for their children.

kvetch (KVETCH): Yiddish for continual complaining.

latke (LOT-kah): Yiddish term for potato pancake traditionally eaten on **Hanukkah.**

l'chaim (luh-KHYE-eem): The traditional Jewish toast before a drink; Hebrew meaning "to life."

machzor (MAKH-zore): A special holiday prayer book, especially that used on the **High Holidays.**

Magen David (mah-GEN dah-VEED): Hebrew term literally meaning "Shield of David," this is the term for the six-pointed Jewish Star. It is sometimes called the Star of David.

Maimonides, Moses (MOH-ses my-MON-eh-dees): Jewish philosopher, commentator, and scholar (1135–1204), also known by the acronym Rambam (Rabbi Moses ben Maimon).

mamzer (MOM-zer): Hebrew for bastard, or illegitimate child.

maror (mah-ROAR): Hebrew name for the bitter herbs served at the Passover **Seder.**

mashiach (mah-SHEE-akh): Hebrew for Messiah, meaning "the anointed one."

matzah (MAH-tsah); pl. **matzot** (mah-TSOTE): Hebrew name for the unleavened bread eaten on Passover.

mazel tov (MAH-zull TOVE): Hebrew expression meaning "Good luck!" or "Congratulations!"

menorah (meh-NOE-rah): A candelabra: nine-branched (eight for the eight days of the holiday and one for lighting the others) for use at **Hanukkah** or seven-branched as the ancient and modern symbol of Israel.

mensch (MENCH): Yiddish for an admirable, upstanding person.

meshugge (meh-SHOO-gah): Yiddish for crazy, silly, nuts, and so forth, often used affectionately.

Messianic Jew or **Jew for Jesus:** Member of a religious movement who believes that she or he is Jewish but holds that Jesus is the Jewish Messiah and God. Messianic Jews are considered by both Judaism and Christianity to be Christians.

mezuzah (meh-ZUH-zah): A small amulet containing a Hebrew scroll that is placed on the doorposts of Jewish homes. Literally "doorpost."

mikveh (MICK-veh): Hebrew term for body of water used for ritual immersion.

milchig (MILL-khick): Yiddish word for foods in the dairy category and therefore not mixable with meat products under the **kosher** laws.

minyan (MIN-yin): Hebrew term for the quorum of ten people needed for certain prayer services.

misheberach (mee-she-BAY-rahkh): Hebrew term literally meaning "May the One who blessed…, this most commonly refers to prayers for healing recited during services.

Mishna (MISH-nah): Hebrew term for the compilation of oral law assembled by Rabbi Yehudah HaNasi in 200 C.E.

Mishne Torah (MISH-neh TOE-rah): A code of Jewish law compiled by **Maimonides** in the twelfth century.

mishpachah (mish-pah-KHAH): Hebrew for family. You may also hear the Yiddish pronunciation: mish-PUH-khah.

mitzvah (MITS-vah); pl. **mitzvot** (mits-VOTE): Hebrew for commandment, this term is also often understood as "a good deed."

mohel (MOE-hel): Hebrew term for one who performs ritual circumcision. You may also hear the Yiddish pronunciation: MOY-el.

nachas (NAH-khiss): A special pride, pleasure, joy, or fulfillment that one gets especially from one's children or grandchildren.

nefesh (NEH-fesh): Hebrew for soul.

ner tamid (NEHR tah-MEED): Hebrew term for the eternal light commonly found surrounding the ark in the synagogue.

nigun (knee-GOON); pl. **nigunim** (knee-goo-NEEM): Hebrew for a wordless melody or tune.

nosh (NOSH): Yiddish word meaning "a snack," or the verb, "to snack."

nu (NU): Yiddish expression meaning "So?" or "Well?" or "Tell me."

nudnik (NOOD-nik): Yiddish for an annoying person.

Oneg Shabbat (oh-NEG shah-BAHT): Hebrew term meaning "delight of the Sabbath," this refers to the informal reception held after Sabbath services.

oy (OY): Popular Yiddish expression/exclamation of woe, surprise, fear, grief. Often heard are **oy vei** (short for **oy vei** is **meir**), "woe is me," and **oy gevalt.**

parasha (pah-rah-SHAH): Hebrew term for the weekly **Torah** reading, also called **parashat ha-shavuah** (pah-rah-SHAHT hah-shah-VOO-ah), literally "portion of the week."

pareve (PAR-ehve): Yiddish word meaning "neutral" used for foods that are neither meat nor dairy and that may be eaten with either.

Pesach (PAY-sakh): Hebrew name for the holiday of Passover.

Purim (POOR-um): Carnival-like spring holiday celebrating the triumph over Haman and the Persian king documented in the biblical book of Esther.

rabbi (RAB-eye): Hebrew term literally meaning "my teacher," this is the title given to the ordained spiritual leader of a Jewish congregation.

Rashi (RAH-shee): Acronym for Rabbi Shlomo ben Isaac (1040–1105), a French Hebrew scholar who commented widely on the Bible and the Talmud.

rebbe (REH-bee): Yiddish term for the charismatic leader of a **Chasidic** group.

rebbetzin (REH-bit-sin): Yiddish term used for the wife of a rabbi.

Rosh Hashanah (ROSH-hah-SHAH-nah): The Jewish New Year and beginning of the **High Holy Days.**

Rosh Hodesh (ROSH-HOE-desh): Minor holiday that occurs at the beginning of each Hebrew month at the time of the new moon.

ruach (ROO-ach): Hebrew for spirit or enthusiasm.

Seder (SAY-der): Hebrew name for traditional Passover meal.

sefer (SAY-fair): Hebrew for book.

sefer Torah (SAY-fair toe-RAH): Hebrew for the sacred, handwritten scroll, containing the first five books of the Bible, which is in the ark at the front of the synagogue.

Sephardim (she-far-DEEM): Hebrew name given to that group of Jews who trace their ancestry to Spain, Portugal, the Mediterranean, North Africa, and the Middle East.

Shabbat (shah-BAHT): Hebrew term for Sabbath.

Shabbat shalom (shah-BAHT shah-LOME): Hebrew greeting used on the Sabbath; literally "Sabbath of peace."

Shabbos (SHA-bis): Yiddish pronunciation of **Shabbat.**

shalom (sha-LOME): Hebrew greeting literally meaning "peace," it is used for hello and goodbye as well.

shanah tovah (SHAH-nah TOE-vah): Traditional Hebrew greeting for Rosh Hashanah meaning "a good year."

Shavuot (shah-VOO-ote): The Feast of Weeks or Pentecost commemorating the giving of the **Torah** at Mt. Sinai.

Shechina (sheh-khee-NAH): A feminine term for God introduced in Talmudic times.

Shehecheyanu (sheh-HEH-khee-YAH-noo): A blessing thanking God for enabling us to reach this moment in time, it is said on holidays and at other joyous events.

sheloshim (sheh-loe-SHEEM): The thirty-day mourning period observed by Jews.

Shema (sheh-MAH): This central prayer of Jewish liturgy coming from the **Torah** (Deut 6:4) reads: "Shema Yisrael Adonai Eloheinu Adonai Echad," meaning "Hear O Israel, **Adonai** is our God, **Adonai** is One."

shiksa (SHICK-sah): Derogatory Yiddish term for non-Jewish woman.

shivah (SHIH-vah): The first, most intense, seven-day period of mourning. Hebrew for seven.

shlemiel (shlih-MEAL): Yiddish for loser.

shlep (SHLEP): Yiddish meaning "to drag or lug."

shlimazel (shlih-MAH-zull): Yiddish for an unlucky person.

shlock (SHLOCK): Yiddish for junk.

shmooze (SHMOOZ): Yiddish for friendly chatting.

shmuck (SCHMUCK): Vulgar Yiddish term for penis; used for an obnoxious person or jerk.

Shoah (SHOW-ah): Hebrew for the Holocaust, literally "destruction."

shochet (SHOW-khet): A ritual slaughterer of animals for **kosher** meat.

shofar (SHOW-far): Hebrew for the hollowed-out animal's (often a ram's) horn blown like a trumpet during the High Holidays.

shtetl (SHTET-ull): Yiddish term for small village.

shul (SHOOL): Yiddish for synagogue.

Siddur (sih-DOOR); pl. **siddurim** (sih-duh-REEM): Hebrew for prayerbook.

simcha (sim-KHAH): Hebrew term for a joyous event.

sivivon (sih-vee-VONE): The Hebrew name for **dreidel.**

spice box: The small perforated box filled with spices that is used during the **Havdalah** ceremony at the close of **Shabbat.**

Star of David: Six-pointed star also known as a Jewish Star or **Magen David.**

sukkah (SUH-kah): Hebrew for small open shack that Jews spend time in on the holiday of **Sukkot.**

Sukkot (soo-COTE): Eight-day harvest holiday that takes place shortly after **Yom Kippur.**

Shulkhan Arukh (shool-KHAN ah-ROOKH): Authoritative code of Jewish Law compiled in 1565 by Joseph Karo.

sofer (soe-FAIR): A scribe trained to inscribe **torah, mezuzah,** and **tefillin** scrolls.

synagogue: Most common term for Jewish house of worship.

tallis (TAH-liss): The Yiddish pronunciation of **tallit.**

tallit (tah-LEET); pl. **tallitot** (tah-lee-TOTE): Fringed prayer shawl.

Talmud (TAHL-muhd): Collection of **Mishna** and commentary from which Modern or Rabbinic Judaism is derived.

Tanach (tah-NACH): Hebrew term for the Jewish Bible, it is an acronym for the three sections that make up the Bible.

Tashlich (TASH-likh): A **Rosh Hashanah** afternoon ceremony in which one's sins are symbolically cast into a body of water.

tefilah (teh-fee-LAH): The Hebrew term for prayer.

tefillin (teh-FILL-in): Small black leather boxes with attached straps worn by traditional Jews for morning, weekday prayers.

Temple: 1. The historic central site of Jewish worship in biblical times, destroyed in 586 B.C.E. and 70 C.E. 2. A synonym for synagogue.

teshuvah (teh-shoo-VAH): Hebrew term meaning repentance.

Tetragrammaton: Greek term used for the four-letter, unpronounceable name of God consisting of the four Hebrew letters, **yod, hay, vov,** and **hay.**

tikkun olam (tee-KOON oh-LAHM): Hebrew for repair of the world.

Torah (toe-RAH): Hebrew term meaning 1. the first five books of the Bible, 2. the actual scroll that is in the ark of the synagogue, 3. all Jewish law and learning.

treif (TRAYF): Yiddish for nonkosher food.

tuchis (TUH-khiss): Yiddish term for buttocks; literally "underneath." Sometimes called tushee (TUSH-ee) or just tush.

tzadik (tsah-DEEK): Hebrew term meaning "righteous one," referring to an especially praiseworthy scholar or person.

tzedakah (tsuh-DOCK-ah): A Hebrew word, literally "righteousness," generally translated as "charity."

tzitzit (TSEET-tseet): The four fringes at the corners of the **tallit.**

Ve-ahavta (veh-ah-HAV-tah): The prayer immediately following the **Shema** in the liturgy.

Wailing Wall or **Western Wall:** The archaeological site in Jerusalem that is the remaining support wall of the ancient Temple, this is considered to be a holy Jewish site. Also called the Kotel (CO-tell).

yahrzeit (YAHR-tsite): Yiddish term for the anniversary of someone's death.

yarmulke (YAAH-mih-kah): Yiddish term for **kippah.**

Yerushalayim (yeh-ROO-shah-LYE-eem): Hebrew term for Jerusalem.

Yiddish (YID-ish): Folk language of **Askenazic** Jews.

Yisra'el (yis-rah-ALE): Hebrew term for Israel.

Yom ha-Shoah (YOME hah-SHOW-ah): Hebrew term for Holocaust Remembrance Day.

Yom Kippur (YOME key-POOR): The Jewish Day of Atonement, a day spent in fasting and prayer; the conclusion of the **High Holidays.**

Zion (ZYE-on): The name of a hill in Jerusalem, this word has come to mean the land of Israel.

Zionism: The term given to the modern political and religious movement to establish a Jewish homeland in the land of Israel.

Zohar (ZOE-har): The ancient book, written in **Aramaic,** which is the central text of Jewish mysticism.

Bibliography

JEWISH THEOLOGY/GENERAL INFORMATION

Kertzer, Morris N., and Lawrence A. Hoffman. *What Is a Jew,* Collier, 1993. An excellent readable introduction to Judaism for Jew and Christian.

Kolatch, Alfred J. *The Jewish Book of Why,* Jonathan David Publishers, 1981, and *The Second Book of Why,* 1985. Widely available and very readable collection of questions and answers about Jewish practice, customs, and the like.

Kushner, Harold S. *How Good Do We Have to Be? A New Understanding of Guilt and Forgiveness,* Little, Brown, 1996. Great discussion of being in relationship with God along with a very different take on what happened in the Garden of Eden.

———. *To Life! A Celebration of Jewish Being and Thinking,* Little, Brown, 1993. A wonderfully upbeat modern view of the joy of taking Judaism seriously.

———. *When Bad Things Happen to Good People,* Avon, 1981 (available widely in paperback). A classic work on the most fundamental problem of religion.

Prager, Dennis, and Joseph Telushkin. *The Nine Questions People Ask About Judaism,* Simon and Schuster, 1981. Simple, direct, compelling analysis of why intelligent, rational people should be religious.

Telushkin, Joseph. *Jewish Literacy,* William Morrow, 1991. A wonderful resource, the book devotes a page to a page and a half on each key topic of Jewish literacy.

Wylen, Stephen M. *Settings of Silver,* Paulist Press, 1989. If you want more detail than Kertzer and Hoffman in an extremely readable volume written for a college-level reader, this is it.

SPIRITUAL APPROACHES

Greenberg, Irving. *The Jewish Way: Living the Holidays,* Summit Books, 1988. A wonderful book that provides deep spiritual insight into *Shabbat* and the Holidays.

Heschel, A. J. *The Sabbath: Its Meaning for Modern Man,* Farrar, Straus and Giroux, 1951. An amazingly beautiful short book on the meaning of the Sabbath.

Kushner, Lawrence. *Invisible Lines of Connection: Sacred Stories of the Ordinary,* Jewish Lights Publishing, 1996. A wonderful, readable collection of stories.

Spitz, Elie K. *Does the Soul Survive?* Jewish Lights Publishing, 2000. Explores Jewish mystical beliefs about reincarnation.

Wolpe, David J. *The Healer of Shattered Hearts: A Jewish View of God,* Henry Holt, 1990. Very deep and moving book about relationship with God.

JEWISH LAW AND SOURCES

Friedman, Richard Elliott. *Who Wrote the Bible?* Harper and Row, 1987. A fascinating look at the documentary hypothesis of the Bible and how it was written.

Gersh, Harry. *The Sacred Books of the Jews,* Stein and Day, 1968. An excellent overview of Jewish sources, including the Bible, the Talmud, the Midrash, commentaries and codes, *responsa,*

Maimonides' *Guide to the Perplexed, kabbalah* and the *Zohar,* and the *Siddur* (prayerbook).

Shapiro, Mark Dov. *Gates of Shabbat,* Central Conference of American Rabbis, 1991. A wonderful guide for Jewish Sabbath observance including how to get started (a little bit at a time).

Stern, Chaim, Editor. *On the Doorposts of Your House,* Central Conference of American Rabbis, 1994. All the prayers for the home with English, Hebrew, transliteration, and commentary.

BIBLE AND TORAH

If you want to get a taste of the degree of commentary and discussion that Jewish tradition invests in the sacred texts, start with one of these three Torah commentaries.

- *The Chumash, Stone Edition,* Mesorah Publications, 1993 (traditional)

- *Etz Hayim: Torah and Commentary,* The Rabbinical Assembly, The Jewish Publication Society, 2001 (Conservative)

- *The Torah; A Modern Commentary,* G. Plaut, Editor, Union of American Hebrew Congregations, 1981 (Reform)

ANTISEMITISM

Cargas, Harry James. *Shadows of Auschwitz: A Christian Response to the Holocaust,* Crossroad, 1992. A very moving discussion of what happened from a Christian perspective. Includes the most powerful commentary on Holocaust photographs that I've ever seen.

Prager, Dennis, and Joseph Telushkin. *Why the Jews: The Reason for Antisemitism,* Simon and Schuster, 1983. More than any other source, this book helped me make sense of this difficult and emotional subject.

Spiegelman, Art. *Maus: A Survivor's Tale,* Pantheon, 1973 (Vol. I) and 1986 (Vol. II). These two volumes tell the story of the author's parents who survived the Holocaust. What makes it unique is that it is done in comic book fashion with the Jews depicted as mice, Nazis as cats, and so on. Not at all childish.

Wiesel, Elie. *Night,* Bantam Books, 1960. Elie Wiesel is a recipient of the Nobel Peace Prize who has published widely on his experience as a Holocaust victim. All his books are moving and insightful.

Wiesenthal, Simon. *The Sunflower: On the Possibilities and Limits of Forgiveness,* Schocken Books, 1998. This moving book tells of Wiesenthal's experience as a concentration camp slave. He was asked to forgive a dying Nazi soldier who had brutally murdered Jews. His refusal and story is interesting and moving but especially so in light of the second part of the book, where a long list of thinkers responds to his refusal to forgive.

INTERFAITH UNDERSTANDING

Dunn, James. D. G. *The Partings of the Ways,* SCM Press and Trinity Press, 1991. A highly respected scholarly discussion of the factors that led to the beginning of Christianity.

Grose, George B., and Benjamin J. Hubbard, Editors. *The Abraham Connection: A Jew, Christian and Muslim in Dialogue,* Cross Cultural Publications, 1994. Expanding the dialogue to a trialogue.

Klenicki, Leon, and Geoffrey Wigoder, Editors. *A Dictionary of the Jewish-Christian Dialogue,* Paulist Press, 1984. Jewish and Christian scholars write brief (two- to three-page) essays on thirty-eight interesting topics.

Magida, Arthur J., Editor. *How to Be a Perfect Stranger: A Guide to Etiquette in Other People's Religious Ceremonies,* Jewish Lights Publishing, 1996 (Vol. 1) and 1997 (Vol. 2). A brief overview of the beliefs and religious ceremonies of thirty-seven different religions.

Sigal, Gerald. *The Jew and the Christian Missionary: A Jewish Response to Missionary Christianity,* KTAV Publishing House, 1981. A Jewish scholar addresses sixty-seven scriptural issues in the Hebrew and Christian scriptures—useful if you are curious as to how Judaism addresses such issues.

HISTORY

Armstrong, Karen. *A History of God,* Ballantine Books, 1993. This is a wonderful history of how ideas about God evolved, focusing on Judaism, Christianity, and Islam.

Johnson, Paul A. *History of the Jews,* HarperPerennial, 1988. There are many excellent books on Jewish history; I have found this one especially helpful.

Wylen, Stephen M. *The Jews in the Time of Jesus,* Paulist Press, 1996. An excellent, readable introduction for those especially interested in these times.

JEWISH HUMOR

Spaulding, Henry D., Editor, *Encyclopedia of Jewish Humor,* Jonathan David Publishers, 1969. A wonderful collection of Jewish jokes and stories.

Telushkin, Joseph. *Jewish Humor: What the Best Jewish Jokes Say About the Jews,* William Morrow, 1992. Great jokes along with interesting analysis.

REFERENCE

Encyclopaedia Judaica, Keter Publishing House Jerusalem Ltd., 1972. The standard reference source for all things Jewish in sixteen large volumes. It is now available on CD-ROM.

Index

Page numbers in italics refer to illustrations.

Leon Klenicki, editor, *Toward A Theological Encounter* (A Stimulus Book, 1991).

John Rousmaniere, *A Bridge to Dialogue: The Story of Jewish-Christian Relations,* edited by James A. Carpenter and Leon Klenicki (A Stimulus Book, 1991).

Michael E. Lodahl, *Shekhinah/Spirit* (A Stimulus Book, 1992).

George M. Smiga, *Pain and Polemic: Anti-Judaism in the Gospels* (A Stimulus Book, 1992).

Eugene J. Fisher, editor, *Interwoven Destinies: Jews and Christians Through the Ages* (A Stimulus Book, 1993).

Anthony Kenny, *Catholics, Jews and the State of Israel* (A Stimulus Book, 1993).

Bernard J. Lee, S.M., *Jesus and the Metaphors of God: The Christs of the New Testament,* Conversation on the Road Not Taken, Vol. 2 (A Stimulus Book, 1993).

Eugene J. Fisher, editor, *Visions of the Other: Jewish and Christian Theologians Assess the Dialogue* (A Stimulus Book, 1995).

Leon Klenicki and Geoffrey Wigoder, editors, *A Dictionary of the Jewish-Christian Dialogue,* Expanded Edition (A Stimulus Book, 1995).

Vincent Martin, *A House Divided: The Parting of the Ways between Synagogue and Church* (A Stimulus Book, 1995).

Philip A. Cunningham and Arthur F. Starr, editors, *Sharing Shalom: A Process for Local Interfaith Dialogue Between Christians and Jews* (A Stimulus Book, 1998).

Frank E. Eakin, Jr., *What Price Prejudice? Christian Antisemitism in America* (A Stimulus Book, 1998).

Ekkehard Schuster and Reinhold Boschert-Kimmig, *Hope Against Hope: Johann Baptist Metz and Elie Wiesel Speak Out on the Holocaust* (A Stimulus Book, 1999).

Mary C. Boys, *Has God Only One Blessing? Judaism as a Source of Christian Understanding* (A Stimulus Book, 2000).

Avery Dulles, S.J., and Leon Klenicki, editors, *The Holocaust, Never to Be Forgotten: Reflections on the Holy See's Document* We Remember (A Stimulus Book, 2000).

Johannes Reuchlin, *Recommendation Whether to Confiscate, Destroy and Burn All Jewish Books: A Classic Treatise against Anti-Semitism,* translated, edited, and with an introduction by Peter Wortsman (A Stimulus Book, 2000).

Philip A. Cunningham, *A Story of Shalom: The Calling of Christians and Jews by a Covenanting God* (A Stimulus Book, 2001).

Philip A. Cunningham, *Sharing the Scriptures,* The Word Set Free, Vol. 1 (A Stimulus Book, 2003).

Dina Wardi, *Auschwitz: Contemporary Jewish and Christian Encounters* (A Stimulus Book, 2003).

STIMULUS BOOKS are developed by the Stimulus Foundation, a not-for-profit organization, and are published by Paulist Press. The Foundation wishes to further the publication of scholarly books on Jewish and Christian topics that are of importance to Judaism and Christianity.

The Stimulus Foundation was established by an erstwhile refugee from Nazi Germany who intends to contribute with these publications to the improvement of communication between Jews and Christians.

Books for publication in this Series will be selected by a committee of the Foundation, and offers of manuscripts and works in progress should be addressed to:

The Stimulus Foundation
c/o Paulist Press
997 Macarthur Boulevard
Mahwah, N.J. 07430
www.paulistpress.com